The Ultimate Guide to Marketing for Real Estate Investors

Real Estate Investing, Volume 12

Jim Pellerin

Published by Jim Pellerin, 2024.

THE ULTIMATE GUIDE TO MARKETING FOR REAL ESTATE INVESTORS

First edition. February 24, 2024.

ISBN: 979-8224707348

Written by Jim Pellerin.

Also by Jim Pellerin

Real Estate Investing

Real Estate Investing Strategies: The Secret to Financial Independence with Real Estate

Real Estate Investing with Lease Options - Investing in Real Estate with No Money Down

Invest Now - The Passive Approach to Winning at Real Estate

The Ultimate Beginners Guide to Real Estate Investing

The 98 Best Real Estate Investing Strategies

The Ultimate Beginners Guide to Wholesale Real Estate Investing

The Ultimate Beginners Guide to Rental Real Estate Investing

The Ultimate Beginners Guide to Fix and Flip Real Estate Investing

The Ultimate Beginners Guide to Private Equity Real Estate Investing

Ultimate Beginners Guide to Real Estate Investing Financing

Building Wealth Through Real Estate - A Beginners Retirement Guide

The Ultimate Guide to Marketing for Real Estate Investors

Watch for more at www.jimpellerin.com.

Table of Contents

The Ultimate Guide to Marketing for Real state Investors

Jim Pellerin

Updated for 2024

Why You Should Read This Book

As a Real Estate Investor, you will need to perform some sort of marketing. Ideally, you should hire someone to do your marketing for you. If you decide you want to do it yourself this book will help get you started.

If you decide to hire someone else to do your marketing for you, this book will help you understand what it is they should be doing.

This book provides an overview of how to get started with Real Estate Investing marketing. As always, this book is NOT a practical approach to real estate marketing and the reader is NOT expected to be able to start marketing in real estate after completing this book.

Introduction

Welcome to *"The Ultimate Guide to Marketing for Real state Investors"* In the dynamic world of real estate, successful investors understand that strategic marketing is the key to unlocking unparalleled opportunities and navigating the challenges of the market. Whether you're a seasoned investor looking to refine your marketing approach or a newcomer eager to make your mark, this book is your comprehensive guide to mastering the art and science of real estate marketing.

Throughout the following chapters, we will delve into the fundamental principles of real estate investing, explore the intricacies of building a powerful brand, and dissect a myriad of online and offline marketing strategies tailored specifically for the real estate industry. From understanding the nuances of different markets to leveraging cutting-edge technologies, each section provides actionable insights, case studies, and practical tips that will empower you to elevate your real estate investment game.

Embark on this journey with an open mind, ready to absorb the knowledge and strategies that will transform your approach to real estate marketing. By the end of this book, you'll not only have a robust understanding of the marketing landscape but also possess the tools and tactics needed to thrive in the competitive world of real estate investing.

Chapter 1: Introduction to Real Estate Investing

Section 1: Overview of Real Estate Investing: The Crucial Role of Marketing

Real estate investing stands as a dynamic and multifaceted field that has captivated individuals seeking to build wealth and financial stability. As an introduction to this intricate domain, it is essential to delve into the fundamental concepts that underpin real estate investing and explore the pivotal role that marketing plays in steering success within this industry.

A. Define Real Estate Investing: Unveiling the Foundations

Real estate investing, at its core, involves the strategic acquisition, ownership, and management of real property with the primary goal of generating returns. It spans a spectrum of investment types, ranging from residential and commercial properties to industrial and retail spaces. Investors in real estate may take diverse approaches, such as long-term property ownership for rental income or short-term strategies like property flipping.

To begin with, let's unravel the concept of real estate investing. At its essence, real estate investing is the art of making money by leveraging properties. This could involve purchasing residential homes, apartment buildings, commercial spaces, or even undeveloped land. Investors may generate income through rental payments, property appreciation, or by participating in real estate development projects.

1. Introducing the Concept of Real Estate Investing

Real estate, as an asset class, has long been considered a tangible and stable investment. Unlike stocks or bonds, real estate offers a physical presence and utility. Investors can derive income through rental payments while potentially benefiting from property value appreciation over time. The spectrum of real estate investments is vast, catering to a diverse range of investor preferences and risk appetites.

2. Highlighting the Various Forms of Real Estate Investments

The diversity within real estate investing is extensive. Residential real estate involves single-family homes, multi-family units, and vacation properties. Commercial real estate comprises office buildings, retail spaces, and industrial facilities. Additionally, investors may explore niche markets such as real estate crowdfunding, real estate investment trusts (REITs), or participate in development projects. Each form of investment carries its unique set of opportunities and challenges.

B. Importance of Marketing in the Real Estate Industry: A Catalyst for Success

In the vast landscape of real estate, marketing emerges as a linchpin that can significantly influence the trajectory of investment endeavors. Marketing is not merely a complementary aspect; rather, it is integral to the success of real estate investors. The ability to effectively market properties can make the difference between a stagnant investment and a flourishing portfolio.

1. Emphasizing the Role of Marketing in Driving Success

Marketing in real estate is not confined to selling homes or filling commercial spaces; it extends to the entire investment lifecycle. From identifying lucrative opportunities to attracting tenants or buyers and creating lasting brand recognition, marketing is the driving force. It is the vehicle through which investors communicate the value proposition of their properties to the target audience.

Successful marketing goes beyond mere transactions; it cultivates relationships and fosters trust. Investors must skillfully position their properties in the market, showcasing the unique features that set them apart. Whether it's highlighting a property's architectural charm, emphasizing its potential for future growth, or showcasing the amenities that enhance its appeal, marketing plays a pivotal role in capturing the attention of potential stakeholders.

2. Showcasing How Effective Marketing Can Influence Investment Outcomes

The impact of effective marketing reverberates throughout the investment journey. A well-executed marketing strategy can expedite the sale or rental process, reduce vacancies, and enhance the overall profitability of real estate investments. By building a strong brand presence, investors can attract a steady stream of interested parties, creating a competitive advantage in the market.

Effective marketing doesn't stop at property promotion; it extends to investor relations and networking. Cultivating a positive public image through strategic marketing efforts can attract potential partners, collaborators, and financing opportunities. In a landscape where relationships often dictate success, the ability to market oneself and one's investment endeavors is a skill that can't be underestimated.

In conclusion, the overview of real estate investing illuminates the diverse avenues available to investors and sets the stage for understanding the critical role of marketing in this domain. As we journey through the chapters that follow, each section will unravel a layer of knowledge, providing insights and strategies to empower real estate investors in navigating the complexities of the market.

Section 2: The Fundamentals of Investment in Real Estate: Unveiling Opportunities and Assessing Risks

As real estate investors embark on their journey to build wealth and secure financial prosperity, a deep understanding of the fundamentals of investment becomes paramount. In this section, we will delve into the diverse types of real estate investments, ranging from the traditional residential and commercial properties to niche opportunities like vacation rentals and fix-and-flip ventures. Additionally, we will scrutinize the crucial aspect of risk and reward assessment, an indispensable process for making informed investment decisions.

A. Types of Real Estate Investments: Navigating a Diverse Landscape

1. Explore Residential, Commercial, and Industrial Real Estate

Real estate investments encompass a broad spectrum of property types, each presenting unique opportunities and considerations. At the foundational level, investors often navigate the terrain of residential, commercial, and industrial real estate.

- **Residential Real Estate:** This category involves properties designed for individuals and families to reside in. It includes single-family homes, multi-family units (such as duplexes or apartment buildings), condominiums, and townhouses. Residential real estate is often considered a stable and reliable investment, driven by the constant demand for housing.

- **Commercial Real Estate:** Commercial properties are intended for business use, encompassing office buildings, retail spaces, hotels, and warehouses. Commercial real estate investments offer the potential for higher returns but may come with increased complexity and risk. The success of such investments often hinges on factors like location, economic trends, and market demand.

- **Industrial Real Estate:** Industrial properties include warehouses, manufacturing facilities, and distribution centers. As the e-commerce industry continues to expand, the demand for industrial real estate has surged. Industrial investments are influenced by factors such as logistics, transportation infrastructure, and economic trends.

2. Discuss Niche Investments Like Vacation Rentals or Fix-and-Flip Properties

Beyond the conventional categories, real estate investors can explore niche opportunities that cater to specific market segments or capitalize on unique strategies.

- **Vacation Rentals:** The rise of platforms like Airbnb has fueled interest in vacation rentals. Investors can purchase properties in tourist destinations and generate income through short-term rentals. While this niche can be lucrative, it comes with the challenges of seasonality, local regulations, and the need for effective property management.

- **Fix-and-Flip Properties:** This strategy involves acquiring distressed properties, renovating them, and selling at a profit. Fix-and-flip investments demand a keen eye for property value, renovation costs, and market trends. Successful execution requires a strategic approach to property selection, renovation, and timing.

B. Risk and Reward Assessment: Navigating the Investment Landscape

1. Evaluate the Inherent Risks in Real Estate Investments

Real estate investments, like any other financial endeavor, are not without risks. Understanding and mitigating these risks are critical to ensuring the success and sustainability of an investment portfolio.

- **Market Risk:** Market fluctuations can impact property values and rental incomes. Economic downturns, shifts in demand, and changes in interest rates can expose investors to market risks.

- **Property-Specific Risks:** Each property carries its own set of risks, including maintenance issues, unexpected repairs, or environmental factors. Conducting thorough due diligence on a property is crucial to identifying and mitigating these risks.

- **Financing Risks:** Utilizing leverage through mortgages introduces financing risks. Interest rate fluctuations and the terms of financing can affect the overall return on investment. Investors must carefully assess their borrowing strategies.

2. Discuss Methods for Assessing Potential Rewards and Returns

While risks are inherent, the potential rewards in real estate investments can be substantial. Assessing these rewards requires a comprehensive understanding of the factors that contribute to a property's profitability.

- **Cash Flow Potential:** Evaluating the property's potential to generate positive cash flow through rental income is a fundamental metric. Positive cash flow ensures that the property covers its operating expenses and debt service.

- **Appreciation:** Property appreciation, or the increase in value over time, contributes to the overall return on investment. Factors such as location, market trends, and development in the vicinity can influence appreciation.

- **Tax Benefits:** Real estate investments often come with tax advantages, including deductions for mortgage interest, property taxes, and depreciation. Understanding and leveraging these benefits can enhance overall returns.

- **Exit Strategies:** Having clear exit strategies is crucial for risk mitigation. Whether through selling, refinancing, or converting a property to another use, investors should plan for multiple scenarios to optimize returns.

In conclusion, the fundamentals of real estate investment encompass a diverse array of property types and investment strategies. From traditional residential and commercial properties to niche opportunities like vacation rentals and fix-and-flip ventures, investors have a myriad of options to consider. Yet, the success of these investments hinges on the meticulous evaluation of risks and rewards, a process that involves navigating market dynamics, property-specific considerations, financing strategies, and potential returns. This section lays the groundwork for investors to embark on their journey with a nuanced understanding of the investment landscape.

Section 3: The Role of Marketing in Real Estate: Navigating the Competitive Landscape and Crafting Effective Strategies

In the realm of real estate, where every property holds a story and every transaction is a significant endeavor, the role of marketing emerges as a linchpin for success. In this section, we will unravel the critical importance of marketing for real estate investors, delving into the competitive nature of the market and how effective marketing can create visibility and opportunities. Additionally, we will provide an overview of an array of marketing strategies, ranging from traditional to digital methods, equipping investors with the tools to navigate the dynamic landscape.

A. Why Marketing is Crucial for Real Estate Investors: Unveiling the Competitive Landscape

1. Highlight the Competitive Nature of the Real Estate Market

The real estate market is inherently competitive, characterized by a constant influx of new properties, changing consumer preferences, and varying economic conditions. In such a landscape, where multiple sellers or landlords vie for the attention of a limited pool of buyers or tenants, effective marketing becomes not just an option but a strategic imperative.

- **Saturation and Choice:** The sheer abundance of available properties in the market often leads to saturation. Buyers or tenants are presented with numerous choices, making it imperative for investors to differentiate their offerings through strategic marketing.

- **Ever-Evolving Consumer Expectations:** Consumer expectations are continually evolving, influenced by trends, lifestyle changes, and market dynamics. Investors must adapt their marketing strategies to resonate with the preferences of their target audience.

- **First Impressions Matter:** In a competitive market, first impressions are critical. Potential buyers or tenants often form opinions based on initial interactions with a property's marketing materials, be it online listings, photographs, or promotional content.

2. Discuss How Effective Marketing Can Create Visibility and Opportunities

In a market where visibility is synonymous with opportunity, effective marketing serves as the catalyst for creating a distinct presence and seizing potential opportunities.

- **Building Brand Visibility:** Effective marketing goes beyond individual property listings; it encompasses building a brand that resonates with the target audience. A strong brand presence creates trust and recognition, influencing the decision-making process of potential clients.

- **Seizing Opportunities in a Dynamic Market:** The real estate market is dynamic, with opportunities arising from various sources such as distressed properties, emerging neighborhoods, or changing market trends. Investors who are adept at marketing can quickly identify and capitalize on these opportunities.

- **Establishing Credibility and Trust:** Trust is a cornerstone in real estate transactions. Effective marketing not only attracts attention but also establishes credibility. This can be achieved through transparent communication, professional branding, and showcasing past successes.

B. Overview of Marketing Strategies: Navigating Traditional and Digital Methods

1. Introduce a Variety of Marketing Strategies Applicable to Real Estate

Real estate marketing is a multifaceted discipline that encompasses a diverse range of strategies tailored to reach and engage the target audience effectively.

- **Online Listings and Platforms:** Leveraging online platforms and listings is a fundamental strategy. This includes utilizing real estate websites, property listing platforms, and social media to showcase properties to a broad audience.

- **Professional Photography and Virtual Tours:** Visual appeal is paramount in real estate. Professional photography and virtual tours enable investors to present properties in the best light, offering potential clients immersive experiences from the comfort of their screens.

- **Networking and Relationship Building:** Establishing and nurturing relationships within the industry is a time-tested strategy. Networking with real estate investors, local businesses, and community members can lead to referrals and collaborative opportunities.

2. Explore Both Traditional and Digital Marketing Methods

The evolution of technology has expanded the horizons of real estate marketing, blending traditional approaches with cutting-edge digital methods.

- **Print Advertising and Direct Mail:** Traditional methods such as print advertising in newspapers, magazines, or direct mail campaigns can still be effective in reaching specific demographics and local audiences.

- **Search Engine Optimization (SEO) and Online Advertising:** Embracing digital strategies, including SEO for online visibility and targeted online advertising, ensures that properties are easily discoverable by potential clients actively searching for real estate solutions.

- **Content Marketing and Social Media Engagement:** Creating valuable content, such as blog posts, articles, and engaging on social media platforms, positions investors as industry experts, fostering trust and attracting a loyal following.

In conclusion, the role of marketing in real estate is instrumental, offering investors a means to stand out in a competitive market, create visibility, and seize opportunities. Understanding the competitive nature of the real estate landscape and adopting effective marketing strategies, whether traditional or digital, empowers investors to navigate the dynamic market successfully.

Section 4: Setting Investment Goals in Real Estate: Charting a Course for Success

In the intricate landscape of real estate investment, the importance of setting clear and strategic goals cannot be overstated. This section delves into the art and science of establishing both short-term and long-term objectives, emphasizing the critical role of aligning these goals with overall investment strategies. Additionally, we explore how marketing, a powerful tool in the investor's arsenal, can be harnessed to tailor campaigns that directly contribute to achieving specific investment goals.

A. Establishing Short-term and Long-term Objectives: A Foundation for Success

1. Define Short-term and Long-term Goals in Real Estate

Real estate investment goals can be broadly categorized into short-term and long-term objectives, each serving a distinct purpose in an investor's journey.

- **Short-term Goals:** Short-term goals typically span one to three years and focus on immediate achievements. These could include securing a certain number of rental properties, completing renovations on a fix-and-flip project, or achieving a specific cash flow target within a defined timeframe.

- **Long-term Goals:** Long-term goals extend beyond the three-year horizon and often encompass broader financial objectives. These might involve building a diversified portfolio, achieving a target net worth, or establishing a real estate investment business with a sustainable revenue stream.

2. Discuss the Importance of Aligning Goals with Overall Investment Strategies

The efficacy of setting goals lies not only in their clarity but also in their alignment with the overarching investment strategy. This synergy ensures that every action taken, including property acquisitions, financing decisions, and marketing initiatives, contributes cohesively to the investor's vision.

- **Strategic Decision-Making:** Aligning goals with overall investment strategies enables strategic decision-making. For instance, an investor with a long-term goal of building a passive income stream might prioritize stable, cash-flowing properties over riskier, high-appreciation ventures.

- **Risk Mitigation:** Clarity in goals facilitates risk mitigation. Investors can assess potential risks through the lens of their objectives, allowing them to make informed decisions that align with their risk tolerance and long-term vision.

- **Consistency in Actions:** An aligned goal and strategy framework ensures consistency in actions. Whether it's property selection, financing choices, or marketing approaches, the investor's decisions remain congruent with the desired outcomes.

B. Aligning Goals with Marketing Strategies: Crafting Purposeful Campaigns

1. Explore How Marketing Can be Tailored to Specific Investment Goals

Marketing serves as a dynamic tool that can be tailored to align with specific investment goals. The versatility of marketing strategies allows investors to craft campaigns that resonate with their short-term and long-term objectives.

- **Goal: Increasing Property Visibility and Occupancy:** Investors aiming to enhance the visibility and occupancy rates of their rental properties can leverage online listings, professional photography, and engaging virtual tours. Targeted social media campaigns can also be employed to reach potential tenants in specific demographics.

- **Goal: Property Appreciation and High Returns:** Investors focused on property appreciation and high returns might employ strategic content marketing. This could include creating content that highlights the potential for property value appreciation, local development projects, and economic trends influencing the market.

- **Goal: Building a Brand and Attracting Investors:** For those with a long-term goal of building a brand and attracting investors, marketing efforts can extend beyond individual properties. Engaging in thought leadership through blogs, webinars, and industry events positions the investor as an expert, attracting potential partners and collaborators.

2. Provide Examples of Goal-Oriented Marketing Campaigns

- **Example 1: Increasing Property Occupancy Rates:** *Campaign Focus:* Utilize targeted online advertising and social media campaigns to showcase the unique features of rental properties. Offer incentives such as limited-time discounts or promotional rates to attract potential tenants quickly.

- **Example 2: Maximizing Property Value Appreciation:** *Campaign Focus:* Develop content marketing materials that emphasize the potential for property appreciation in specific neighborhoods or regions. Utilize SEO strategies to ensure that the content is discoverable by individuals actively searching for investment opportunities.

- **Example 3: Building a Brand and Attracting Investors:** *Campaign Focus:* Engage in content creation across multiple channels, including blog posts, webinars, and participation in industry events. Showcase past successful projects, share insights into market trends, and position oneself as an authority in real estate investment.

In conclusion, setting investment goals in real estate serves as the compass guiding investors through the complexities of the market. Whether short-term or long-term, these goals provide a roadmap for strategic decision-making and risk management. Aligning these goals with marketing strategies empowers investors to craft purposeful campaigns that directly contribute to the realization of their objectives. As we venture further into the realms of real estate investment, subsequent sections will delve into specific marketing strategies, providing actionable insights for investors to optimize their campaigns and achieve their desired outcomes.

Section 5: Case Studies: Real-world Lessons in

Real Estate Success

Real estate investing is not a one-size-fits-all venture; it's a dynamic field where success stories unfold through various paths and strategies. In this section, we will delve into real-world examples of successful real estate investors, showcasing their diverse journeys across different markets. Additionally, we will analyze the pivotal role of marketing in their success, extracting valuable lessons and principles that readers can apply to their own investment endeavors.

A. Real-world Examples of Successful Real Estate Investors: A Mosaic of Paths to Success

1. Showcase Diverse Investors Across Different Markets:

Success in real estate knows no geographical boundaries or singular methodologies. By exploring the stories of diverse investors across various markets, we gain insights into the adaptability and creativity that characterize triumphs in this field.

- **Case Study 1: Urban Redevelopment Maven in New York City:** Meet Alex Rodriguez, a real estate investor based in New York City, who specializes in urban redevelopment projects. By identifying undervalued properties in burgeoning neighborhoods, Rodriguez has successfully transformed neglected buildings into sought-after residential spaces, capitalizing on the city's ever-evolving landscape.

- **Case Study 2: Suburban Real Estate Tycoon in the Midwest**: Sarah Johnson, a seasoned investor in the Midwest, has carved her niche in suburban real estate. Leveraging her knowledge of local trends and preferences, Johnson has built a portfolio of family-friendly properties, focusing on long-term rental income and property appreciation.

- **Case Study 3: Vacation Property Maestro in Coastal Destinations**: Mark Thompson, with a passion for coastal living, has strategically invested in vacation properties in prime coastal destinations. His success lies in understanding the seasonal nature of these markets, creating alluring listings, and maximizing short-term rental income.

2. Highlight Various Paths to Success in Real Estate Investing

Each investor's journey is unique, shaped by individual goals, market dynamics, and personal preferences. By examining these diverse paths to success, readers can gain inspiration and identify strategies that resonate with their own aspirations.

- **Adaptability and Market Awareness:** Successful investors showcase a keen awareness of market trends and adaptability to changing conditions. Whether it's recognizing emerging neighborhoods, understanding demographic shifts, or predicting economic changes, staying attuned to the market is a common thread.

- **Risk-Taking and Innovation:** Many success stories in real estate involve an element of risk-taking and innovation. Investors who are willing to explore unconventional strategies, such as redevelopment projects or niche markets, often find themselves at the forefront of lucrative opportunities.

- **Long-term Vision and Planning:** Building wealth through real estate requires a long-term vision and strategic planning. Investors who focus on sustainable growth, consider future market trends, and employ sound financial planning often outperform their short-term-focused counterparts.

B. Highlighting the Role of Marketing in Their Success: Extracting Valuable Lessons for Readers

1. Analyze Specific Marketing Strategies Employed by Successful Investors

The success of real estate investors is not solely attributed to property selection or financial acumen; marketing plays a pivotal role in amplifying their achievements. By dissecting the marketing strategies of these successful investors, we can identify key principles that contributed to their triumphs.

- **Strategic Property Positioning:** In the competitive real estate landscape, successful investors strategically position their properties. This involves not just showcasing physical attributes but also creating a narrative that resonates with the target audience. For instance, Alex Rodriguez in New York City focuses on the historical charm and cultural significance of his redevelopment projects.

- **Digital Presence and Online Marketing:** The digital era has transformed the way properties are marketed. Successful investors leverage online platforms, websites, and social media to create a compelling digital presence. Sarah Johnson in the Midwest, for example, utilizes professional photography and engaging content on social media to attract potential tenants.

- **Community Engagement and Networking:** Real estate is not just about properties; it's about people and communities. Mark Thompson, specializing in vacation properties, actively engages with the local communities of coastal destinations. This involvement not only enhances the appeal of his properties but also builds trust within the community.

2. Extract Lessons and Principles from These Case Studies for Readers to Apply

The success stories of these investors offer valuable lessons and principles that readers can apply to their own real estate journeys. These lessons extend beyond marketing and encompass broader strategies for building a robust and resilient investment portfolio.

- **Lesson 1: Tailor Your Approach to the Market:** Successful investors understand that a one-size-fits-all strategy doesn't work in real estate. Tailoring your approach to the specific characteristics and demands of your target market is crucial. Whether it's adapting to urban redevelopment, suburban family living, or vacation property markets, aligning with local dynamics is key.

- **Lesson 2: Embrace Creativity and Innovation:** Innovation and creativity are catalysts for success in real estate. Whether it's reimagining neglected urban spaces or identifying unique niches like coastal vacation properties, successful investors embrace creativity and bring innovative solutions to the market.

- **Lesson 3: Build and Leverage Your Brand:** Building a recognizable and trustworthy brand is a recurring theme among successful investors. Marketing extends beyond individual properties; it involves crafting a brand identity that resonates with the target audience. This brand-building creates a lasting impact and contributes to long-term success.

- **Lesson 4: Incorporate Technology and Digital Marketing:** The digital era has transformed the way real estate is marketed. Successful investors leverage technology, including online listings, virtual tours, and social media, to enhance their marketing efforts. Embracing digital tools and staying ahead of technological trends is crucial in today's competitive landscape.

- **Lesson 5: Focus on Long-term Sustainability:** Building wealth through real estate requires a focus on long-term sustainability. Successful investors plan for the future, consider market trends, and implement sound financial strategies. This long-term vision ensures resilience and the ability to weather market fluctuations.

In conclusion, the case studies of successful real estate investors offer a rich tapestry of experiences, strategies, and lessons. By exploring the diverse journeys of investors in different markets, readers can gain inspiration and insights into the adaptable and innovative approaches that lead to success. The role of marketing is not just a supporting element but a driving force behind their achievements, underscoring its significance in the competitive and dynamic landscape of real estate investing.

Chapter 2: Building Your Brand

Section 1: Branding Basics: Crafting a Distinct Identity in Real Estate Investing

In the competitive realm of real estate investing, where every property competes for attention, establishing a strong and recognizable brand is not just a marketing strategy; it's a cornerstone of success. This section will delve into the fundamentals of branding, exploring how investors can define their brand identity and why cultivating a strong brand is crucial in the dynamic landscape of real estate.

A. Defining Your Brand Identity: Clarifying the Elements

At its essence, brand identity is the unique set of characteristics and attributes that distinguish a business or individual from others in the market. In the context of real estate investing, where trust and credibility play pivotal roles, defining a clear and compelling brand identity is instrumental.

1. Clarify the Elements that Constitute a Brand Identity

A brand identity encompasses a variety of elements that collectively shape how a business is perceived. These elements include:

- **Logo and Visual Elements:** The visual representation of your brand, including logos, color schemes, and design elements, creates an immediate and lasting impression. A well-designed logo can serve as a visual anchor for your brand.

- **Brand Voice and Messaging:** The way you communicate, both in written and spoken form, contributes to your brand identity. Whether your messaging is formal, casual, or innovative, it should align with your target audience and market positioning.

- **Values and Mission:** Clearly articulating the values and mission of your real estate investment business establishes a foundation for your brand. This can include a commitment to transparency, community engagement, or a specific investment philosophy.

- **Consistency Across Platforms:** Consistency is key in brand identity. Whether someone encounters your brand on a social media platform, a property listing, or a business card, the experience should be cohesive and reflective of your brand.

2. Discuss the Significance of a Unique and Recognizable Brand

A unique and recognizable brand is a powerful asset in the competitive landscape of real estate investing. Here's why:

- **Differentiation in a Crowded Market:** The real estate market is saturated with properties and investors. A distinctive brand helps you stand out in this crowded market, making it easier for potential clients and partners to remember and choose you.

- **Building Trust and Credibility:** A consistent and well-defined brand builds trust. When clients and partners encounter a brand that is clear about its values and mission, it instills confidence and credibility.

- **Memorability and Recall:** A memorable brand is more likely to be recalled when opportunities arise. Whether it's a referral from a previous client or a potential partnership, a strong brand increases the likelihood of being top-of-mind.

B. Importance of a Strong Brand in Real Estate Investing: Enhancing Credibility and Attracting Opportunities

Explore How a Strong Brand Enhances Credibility

Credibility is a currency in real estate investing, where significant financial transactions and long-term relationships are at stake. A strong brand contributes to credibility in several ways:

- **Professionalism and Trustworthiness:** A well-designed and consistently presented brand conveys professionalism and trustworthiness. This is particularly crucial in real estate, where clients seek assurance in their investment decisions.

- **Consistency in Service and Experience:** A strong brand sets expectations. When clients and partners have a clear understanding of your brand, they know what to expect in terms of service, communication, and overall experience. Consistency in delivering on these expectations builds trust.

- **Positioning as an Industry Expert:** A brand that reflects expertise and authority in real estate investing positions you as an industry leader. This can attract clients who are seeking knowledgeable and experienced partners for their investment journey.

2. Discuss the Impact of Branding on Attracting Clients and Partners

In the collaborative landscape of real estate, attracting clients and forming partnerships is a continuous process. A strong brand plays a pivotal role in these interactions:

- **Attracting the Right Clients:** A well-defined brand attracts clients who resonate with your values and investment approach. This alignment enhances the likelihood of successful and enduring partnerships.

- **Building a Network of Partnerships:** Real estate investing often involves collaborations with various stakeholders, including real estate agents, contractors, and financing partners. A strong brand can attract like-minded professionals and foster mutually beneficial partnerships.

- **Facilitating Referrals and Word-of-Mouth Marketing:** A memorable brand encourages satisfied clients and partners to refer your services. Word-of-mouth marketing is a powerful force in real estate, and a strong brand amplifies this organic promotion.

In conclusion, the fundamentals of branding in real estate investing go beyond visual elements and extend to the values, consistency, and experience associated with your brand. A strong and recognizable brand is not just an asset; it's a strategic advantage that differentiates you in a competitive market, enhances credibility, and attracts the right clients and partners.

Section 2: Creating a Professional Online Presence in Real Estate Investing

In the digital age, establishing a robust online presence is not just an option; it's a necessity for success in real estate investing. This section will delve into the strategies and best practices for creating a professional online presence, focusing on website development and optimization, as well as utilizing social media for brand building.

A. Website Development and Optimization: Building the Digital Foundation

1. Highlight the Key Elements of an Effective Real Estate Website

A well-crafted website serves as the digital storefront for real estate investors. It's the first point of contact for potential clients and partners, making it crucial to create a positive and informative user experience.

- **User-Friendly Design:** The design of a real estate website should prioritize user-friendliness. Intuitive navigation, clear calls-to-action, and a visually appealing layout contribute to a positive user experience.

- **Property Listings and Descriptions:** Property listings are the core content of a real estate website. Each listing should feature high-quality visuals, detailed property descriptions, and relevant information such as price, location, and amenities.

- **Contact and Inquiry Forms:** Facilitating communication is essential. Contact forms and inquiry options should be easily accessible, encouraging visitors to reach out with questions or express interest in properties.

- **Mobile Responsiveness:** With the prevalence of mobile devices, ensuring that a real estate website is responsive on various screen sizes is imperative. Mobile-friendly design enhances accessibility and user engagement.

2. Discuss Strategies for Optimizing Websites for User Experience and Search Engines

Optimizing a real estate website involves aligning it with both user expectations and search engine algorithms. This dual optimization enhances visibility and ensures that the website effectively serves its purpose.

- **SEO (Search Engine Optimization):** SEO is a fundamental aspect of website optimization. This involves optimizing content, meta tags, and other elements to improve the website's ranking on search engine results pages. Keyword research, local SEO, and relevant content creation contribute to effective SEO strategies.

- **Loading Speed and Performance:** The speed at which a website loads significantly impacts user satisfaction and search engine rankings. Optimizing images, utilizing caching, and choosing a reliable hosting service contribute to faster loading times.

- **Clear Call-to-Action (CTA):** A clear and compelling call-to-action guides visitors on the desired actions, whether it's filling out a contact form, scheduling a consultation, or exploring property listings. CTAs should be strategically placed throughout the website.

- **Analytics and Data Tracking:** Utilizing analytics tools helps in tracking user behavior, popular content, and areas for improvement. This data-driven approach allows real estate investors to refine their websites based on actual user interactions.

B. Utilizing Social Media for Brand Building: Expanding Reach and Engagement

1. Explore Platforms Suitable for Real estate investors

Social media platforms offer real estate investors powerful tools for brand building, audience engagement, and networking. Choosing the right platforms is essential to reach the target audience effectively.

- **LinkedIn for Professional Networking:** LinkedIn is a valuable platform for real estate investors. It facilitates professional networking, allows for showcasing expertise through articles and posts, and provides a platform for connecting with potential partners and clients.

- **Instagram for Visual Storytelling:** Instagram is a visual-centric platform, making it ideal for showcasing property listings through high-quality images and videos. Additionally, features like Instagram Stories offer opportunities for real-time updates and behind-the-scenes content.

- **Facebook for Community Engagement:** With its expansive user base, Facebook is a versatile platform for real estate investors. It allows for community engagement through business pages, groups, and targeted advertising. Facebook Live and events can be utilized for virtual property tours and educational sessions.

2. Discuss Content Strategies and Engagement Techniques for Social Media

Effective social media marketing involves more than just posting property listings. It's about creating engaging content that resonates with the audience, building a community, and fostering meaningful interactions.

- **Content Calendar and Consistency:** Establishing a content calendar ensures a consistent and strategic approach to social media. Consistency in posting, whether it's property highlights, market updates, or educational content, keeps the audience engaged.

- **Visual Storytelling with Multimedia:** Visual content, including images, videos, and infographics, is highly effective in capturing attention on social media. Real estate investors can leverage multimedia to tell compelling stories about properties, market trends, and industry insights.

- **Interactive Features and Polls:** Adding interactive elements such as polls, quizzes, and Q&A sessions fosters engagement. It encourages followers to actively participate and provides valuable insights into their preferences and interests.

- **Community Building and Networking:** Social media is not just a broadcasting platform; it's a space for building communities. Real estate investors can actively engage with followers, respond to comments, and participate in industry discussions to strengthen their online presence.

In conclusion, creating a professional online presence in real estate investing involves strategic website development and optimization, coupled with effective utilization of social media platforms. A well-designed website serves as the digital face of a real estate business, offering an intuitive user experience and optimized content for both users and search engines. Social media, on the other hand, presents opportunities for brand building, community engagement and networking.

Section 3: Networking Strategies in Real Estate Investing: Building Connections for Success

Networking is a cornerstone of success in the dynamic world of real estate investing. In this section, we will delve into effective networking strategies, focusing on building relationships with industry professionals and leveraging networking events and platforms. Establishing and maintaining connections within the real estate ecosystem is not just about exchanging business cards; it's a strategic investment that can yield valuable opportunities, insights, and collaborations.

A. Building Relationships with Industry Professionals: The Bedrock of Success

1. Explore the Importance of Networking in Real Estate

Networking is more than a social activity; it's a fundamental aspect of success in real estate investing. The real estate industry thrives on relationships, and effective networking can open doors to new opportunities, partnerships, and insights.

- **Access to Opportunities:** Networking provides access to a wealth of opportunities that might not be readily available through traditional channels. From off-market deals to potential partnerships, networking expands the scope of possibilities.

- **Insights and Market Knowledge:** Building relationships with industry professionals allows real estate investors to tap into valuable insights and market knowledge. Conversations with colleagues, real estate agents, and other professionals provide a nuanced understanding of market trends and opportunities.

- **Establishing a Reputation:** Networking contributes to the establishment of a positive reputation within the industry. Word-of-mouth recommendations and referrals from trusted colleagues can significantly enhance credibility and attract potential clients and partners.

2. Provide Tips on Establishing and Maintaining Professional Relationships

Building successful relationships in real estate involves more than casual interactions. It requires a strategic and genuine approach to establishing and maintaining connections.

- **Be Genuine and Authentic:** Authenticity is key in networking. Building connections based on genuine interactions fosters trust and sets the foundation for long-lasting relationships. Authenticity involves being transparent about goals, values, and areas of expertise.

- **Active Listening:** Effective networking is not just about talking; it's about listening. Actively listening to colleagues, industry professionals, and potential partners demonstrates respect and interest in their perspectives.

- **Provide Value:** Networking is a two-way street. Offering value to others, whether it's through sharing insights, making introductions, or providing resources, strengthens relationships. Being a valuable resource within the network builds credibility and reciprocity.

- **Follow-Up and Nurture Connections:** After initial interactions, following up and nurturing connections is crucial. Sending a personalized follow-up email, connecting on professional social media platforms, or arranging a follow-up meeting demonstrates commitment to the relationship.

B. Leveraging Networking Events and Platforms: Maximizing Opportunities

1. Discuss the Value of Industry Events, Both Online and Offline

Industry events, whether held in person or virtually, offer unparalleled opportunities for networking. These events bring together professionals, investors, and experts, creating a conducive environment for relationship-building.

- **In-Person Networking Events:** In-person events, such as conferences, seminars, and workshops, provide a platform for face-to-face interactions. These events allow for more personal connections, casual conversations, and the chance to showcase expertise.

- **Virtual Networking Platforms:** In the era of digital connectivity, virtual networking platforms have become increasingly prominent. Online events, webinars, and virtual conferences enable professionals to connect from anywhere in the world, expanding the reach of networking efforts.

2. Provide Guidance on Effective Participation in Networking Platforms

Effectively leveraging networking events, whether in person or online, requires a strategic approach. Simply attending events is not enough; active and purposeful participation is key.

- **Set Clear Goals for Networking:** Before attending an event, it's essential to set clear goals for networking. Whether the objective is to connect with potential partners, learn from industry experts, or explore new markets, having defined goals helps in strategic networking.

- **Utilize Digital Platforms for Visibility:** In virtual networking, visibility is crucial. Utilizing digital platforms such as LinkedIn, industry forums, and virtual event platforms enhances visibility and facilitates connections. An updated and professional online presence is an extension of networking efforts.

- **Engage in Thoughtful Conversations:** During networking events, engaging in thoughtful conversations is more impactful than collecting a multitude of business cards. Asking insightful questions, sharing experiences, and actively participating in discussions contribute to meaningful connections.

- **Follow Up Promptly After Events:** The window of opportunity after a networking event is limited. Following up promptly with new connections through personalized messages, invitations to connect on professional platforms, or arranging follow-up meetings ensures that the relationship continues to develop.

In conclusion, networking strategies are integral to success in real estate investing. Building relationships with industry professionals and effectively leveraging networking events and platforms can unlock a myriad of opportunities and contribute to long-term success. The art of networking extends beyond transactions; it's about fostering genuine connections that mutually benefit all parties involved.

Section 4: Establishing Credibility in Real Estate Investing

In the dynamic world of real estate investing, credibility is a currency that holds immense value. Establishing and maintaining credibility goes beyond the tangible aspects of a property; it involves showcasing expertise, building trust, and leveraging positive client experiences. This section will delve into two key aspects of credibility building: showcasing expertise through content creation and utilizing testimonials and reviews to reinforce a positive reputation.

A. Showcasing Expertise Through Content Creation: Positioning Yourself as an Authority

1. Discuss the Role of Content in Establishing Expertise

In an information-driven era, where potential clients and partners seek knowledge and guidance, content creation becomes a powerful tool for real estate investors. Creating and sharing valuable content positions investors as authorities in their field.

- **Educational Blog Posts:** Maintaining a blog on your website allows you to share in-depth insights into various aspects of real estate investing. Educational blog posts can cover topics such as market trends, investment strategies, and tips for first-time investors.

- **Informative Videos and Webinars:** Video content has become increasingly popular and effective in conveying complex information. Creating informative videos or hosting webinars on platforms like YouTube or Zoom enables you to reach a broader audience and establish your expertise visually.

- **Engaging Podcasts:** Podcasts provide a platform for in-depth discussions and interviews. Hosting a real estate-focused podcast allows you to share your insights, interview industry experts, and connect with your audience in an audio format.

- **Whitepapers and Research Studies:** Conducting and publishing research studies or whitepapers on relevant real estate topics adds a layer of authority to your brand. This demonstrates a commitment to staying informed about industry trends and contributing valuable insights.

2. Explore Various Content Formats: Blogs, Videos, and Podcasts

The diversity of content formats ensures that your expertise is communicated effectively to a wide range of audiences. Each format has its unique advantages, and incorporating a mix of them into your content strategy maximizes your reach.

- **Blogs for In-Depth Analysis:** Blog posts allow for detailed exploration of topics. They are ideal for conveying comprehensive information, sharing personal experiences, and offering practical advice.

- **Videos for Visual Engagement:** Videos appeal to visual and auditory learners. Whether it's virtual property tours, market updates, or expert interviews, videos enhance engagement and create a more personal connection with your audience.

- **Podcasts for Audio Insights:** Podcasts cater to those who prefer consuming content passively. Through interviews, discussions, and solo episodes, you can share your expertise in a conversational and accessible format.

- **Infographics for Quick Insights:** Infographics are excellent for distilling complex information into visually appealing, digestible formats. They are highly shareable and can convey key insights at a glance.

B. Testimonials and Reviews: Harnessing the Power of Positive Experiences

1. Highlight the Significance of Client Testimonials

Testimonials serve as social proof of your capabilities and the positive experiences of your clients. They are a testament to your credibility and play a crucial role in building trust with potential clients.

- **Building Trust Through Authentic Experiences:** Testimonials go beyond stating facts; they encapsulate the authentic experiences of clients. When potential clients see positive testimonials, they are more likely to trust your services and feel confident in their decision to work with you.

- **Differentiating Your Business:** In a crowded real estate market, client testimonials differentiate your business. They provide a human element to your brand, showcasing the positive impact you've had on clients' lives and investments.

- **Addressing Common Concerns:** Testimonials can address common concerns or reservations potential clients may have. Positive testimonials that highlight successful outcomes and satisfied clients can alleviate doubts and instill confidence.

2. Provide Strategies for Collecting and Leveraging Positive Reviews

Collecting and leveraging positive reviews requires a proactive approach. Satisfied clients may not always volunteer their experiences, but encouraging and facilitating the review process can amplify the impact of positive testimonials.

- **Timely Request for Feedback:** After successfully closing a deal or completing a project, promptly request feedback from clients. Timing is crucial, as clients are likely to provide more detailed and enthusiastic testimonials when their positive experiences are fresh in their minds.

- **Diversify Review Platforms:** Encourage clients to leave reviews on various platforms, including Google, Yelp, and industry-specific websites. Diversifying review sources enhances your online presence and credibility across different online spaces.

- **Incentivize Reviews Responsibly:** While incentivizing reviews can be effective, it's essential to approach this practice ethically. Ensure that incentives are reasonable, transparent, and comply with any regulations or guidelines.

- **Utilize Testimonials Across Marketing Channels:** Once you have a collection of positive testimonials, strategically integrate them into your marketing materials. Feature them on your website, in promotional materials, and within your social media content to consistently reinforce your credibility.

In conclusion, establishing credibility in real estate investing involves a multi-faceted approach that combines showcasing expertise through diverse content creation and harnessing the power of positive client testimonials. By consistently producing valuable content across various formats and actively collecting and leveraging testimonials, real estate investors can build a reputation as trusted authorities in their field. This credibility not only attracts potential clients and partners but also strengthens the foundation for long-term success in the competitive landscape of real estate.

Section 5: Brand Evolution: Navigating the Dynamics of Real Estate

Building a brand in the realm of real estate investing is not a static process; it's an evolutionary journey. As markets shift, trends emerge, and consumer expectations evolve, successful real estate investors recognize the importance of adapting and refining their brands over time. This section will explore the imperative of brand evolution, emphasizing the need for continuous refinement and the role of feedback as a compass for improvement.

A. Adapting and Refining Your Brand Over Time: The Imperative of Evolution

1. Discuss the Need for Brands to Evolve with Market Trends

In the dynamic landscape of real estate, where market trends, consumer behaviors, and industry dynamics are in constant flux, the ability to adapt and evolve is a strategic necessity.

- **Market Sensitivity:** Real estate markets are sensitive to economic, social, and technological changes. Successful brands in real estate stay attuned to these shifts and adjust their messaging, positioning, and offerings accordingly.

- **Consumer Expectations:** As consumer expectations evolve, brands must keep pace. Whether it's changes in preferences, technological adoption, or sustainability concerns, aligning with evolving consumer expectations is pivotal for brand relevance.

- **Competitive Dynamics:** The competitive landscape in real estate is fierce. Brands that continually assess and respond to the strategies of competitors position themselves for sustained success. This involves not only differentiation but also staying ahead of emerging market players.

- **Technological Advancements:** Technology plays a transformative role in real estate. Brands that embrace technological advancements, whether in marketing strategies, customer engagement, or operational efficiency, gain a competitive edge.

2. Explore Examples of Successful Brand Evolutions in Real Estate

Examining real-world examples of brand evolutions in real estate provides insights into the strategies employed by successful investors to stay relevant and resilient.

- **Repositioning for a New Market Landscape:** Consider a real estate investor who initially focused on traditional residential properties but, in response to market demand for sustainable living, evolved their brand to specialize in eco-friendly and energy-efficient homes.

- **Embracing Digital Transformation:** In an era where digital presence is paramount, a real estate investor may undergo a brand evolution by enhancing their online platforms, incorporating virtual reality property tours, and leveraging advanced analytics for personalized client experiences.

- **Catering to Emerging Trends:** A brand evolution might involve aligning with emerging trends, such as the rise of remote work. Investors could adapt their brand messaging to highlight properties suitable for remote living or investment opportunities in regions with a growing remote workforce.

B. Incorporating Feedback for Continuous Improvement: The Feedback Loop

1. Emphasize the Role of Feedback in Brand Refinement

Feedback is the compass that guides brand refinement. Whether it comes from clients, partners, or internal assessments, feedback provides invaluable insights into what is working well, what needs improvement, and how the brand is perceived in the market.

- **Client Satisfaction Surveys:** Regularly conducting client satisfaction surveys is a proactive way to gather feedback. These surveys can delve into aspects such as communication effectiveness, service quality, and overall client experience.

- **Monitoring Online Reviews:** Online reviews on platforms like Google, Yelp, and social media offer a public-facing view of client experiences. Monitoring and responding to these reviews not only address individual concerns but also demonstrate a commitment to client satisfaction.

- **Internal Assessments and Team Feedback:** Internal assessments involve gathering feedback from team members. Their perspectives on brand messaging, collaboration, and operational processes provide a holistic view that can inform strategic refinements.

- **Competitor Analysis:** Analyzing the strategies and successes of competitors contributes to a comprehensive feedback loop. It helps identify areas where the brand can differentiate itself, learn from industry best practices, and stay ahead of evolving market dynamics.

2. Provide a Framework for Gathering and Analyzing Feedback

Gathering feedback is only the first step; effective analysis and implementation of insights are crucial for meaningful brand refinement.

- **Establishing Clear Objectives:** Clearly defining the objectives of gathering feedback sets the foundation for effective analysis. Whether it's improving client satisfaction, refining brand messaging, or adapting to market trends, objectives provide focus.

- **Utilizing Feedback Channels:** Diversifying feedback channels ensures a comprehensive understanding. From direct client interactions to online surveys and social media listening, each channel provides unique insights into different facets of the brand.

- **Quantitative and Qualitative Analysis:** Combining quantitative data, such as numerical ratings and metrics, with qualitative insights from open-ended questions or narrative feedback offers a balanced understanding. This dual analysis allows for both statistical trends and nuanced perspectives.

- **Iterative Implementation:** Implementing feedback is an iterative process. Instead of approaching it as a one-time activity, real estate investors should view feedback implementation as an ongoing cycle of refinement, adapting strategies based on continuous insights.

In conclusion, brand evolution in real estate investing is a dynamic process that involves adapting to market trends, aligning with consumer expectations, and staying ahead of the competition. By recognizing the imperative of evolution and actively seeking feedback for continuous improvement, real estate investors can position their brands as resilient, relevant, and responsive to the ever-changing dynamics of the industry. Whether through repositioning strategies, embracing technological advancements, or aligning with emerging trends, successful brand evolution is a strategic journey that navigates the complexities of the real estate landscape.

Chapter 3: Targeting the Right Markets

Section 1: Market Research - Unveiling the Path to Profitable Real Estate Investments

Market research stands as the cornerstone of successful real estate investing, guiding investors towards high-opportunity areas and informing strategic decisions. This section will delve into the intricate process of market research, exploring techniques for identifying profitable markets and analyzing key factors such as demographics and economic trends.

A. Identifying Profitable Markets: Techniques for Assessing Potential Profitability

1. Techniques for Assessing Market Potential

Successful real estate investors possess the ability to identify markets with the potential for profitability. Various techniques can be employed to assess and gauge the attractiveness of different markets.

- **Supply and Demand Dynamics:** Analyzing the balance between supply and demand is fundamental. Markets with a high demand for real estate but limited supply are often lucrative. Conversely, oversaturated markets may pose challenges unless specific niches or emerging trends are identified.

- **Job Market and Employment Opportunities:** The job market is a key determinant of a region's economic health. Markets with robust job growth and diverse employment opportunities tend to attract a steady influx of residents, creating demand for housing and real estate investments.

- **Infrastructure Development:** The presence and planned development of infrastructure, such as transportation networks, schools, and amenities, can significantly impact a market's attractiveness. Infrastructure improvements often correlate with increased property values.

- **Market Saturation and Competition Analysis:** Conducting a thorough analysis of existing real estate in a market helps gauge saturation and identify areas with less competition. This analysis extends beyond property availability to encompass factors like rental rates and property types.

- **Emerging Trends and Future Projections:** Identifying emerging trends and understanding future projections is crucial. Markets positioned for growth, whether due to demographic shifts, economic investments, or urban development plans, present opportunities for investors.

2. Utilizing Market Data and Trends to Identify High-Opportunity Areas

Market data serves as a treasure trove of insights, guiding investors towards high-opportunity areas. Leveraging available data and staying attuned to market trends are essential practices.

- **Real Estate Market Reports and Analysis:** Regularly reviewing real estate market reports and analyses provides a comprehensive overview of current trends, price movements, and emerging opportunities. Reports from reputable sources offer data-driven insights.

- **Demographic Mapping and Target Audience Profiling:** Demographic mapping involves visualizing and analyzing data related to population characteristics. By understanding the demographics of an area, investors can tailor their strategies to the needs and preferences of the target audience.

- **Economic Indicators and Performance Metrics:** Economic indicators, such as GDP growth, employment rates, and consumer spending, offer a macro-level view of a market's economic health. These metrics help investors assess the overall stability and growth potential of a region.

- **Analyzing Rental Yields and Property Appreciation:** Rental yields and property appreciation rates provide valuable insights into the potential returns on investment. Markets with consistent rental income and appreciating property values are often attractive to investors seeking long-term gains.

B. Analyzing Demographic and Economic Trends: Navigating the Landscape of Market Viability

1. The Role of Demographics in Market Selection

Demographics play a pivotal role in shaping market dynamics. Understanding the composition of a population, their preferences, and lifestyle choices aids investors in selecting markets aligned with their investment goals.

- **Population Growth and Migration Patterns:** Markets experiencing population growth or attracting significant migration are indicative of vitality. Investors may target areas with an influx of residents, translating into increased demand for housing and real estate services.

- **Age Groups and Lifestyle Preferences:** Different age groups have distinct preferences and requirements when it comes to housing. Analyzing demographics helps investors align their strategies with the needs of specific age cohorts, whether it's catering to millennials seeking urban living or retirees looking for tranquil communities.

- **Income Levels and Affordability:** Understanding income levels and affordability is crucial. Investors can tailor their offerings to match the income demographics of a market, ensuring that properties align with the financial capacities of potential buyers or renters.

2. Assessing Economic Indicators for Market Viability

Economic indicators serve as barometers of a market's viability. Analyzing these indicators provides a comprehensive understanding of the economic health and potential risks associated with a particular market.

- **GDP Growth and Economic Stability:** Markets with steady GDP growth and economic stability are attractive to investors. Economic stability contributes to a positive investment environment, reducing the likelihood of volatility impacting real estate values.

- **Employment Rates and Job Diversity:** Markets with low unemployment rates and diverse job opportunities are favorable for real estate investments. Employment stability ensures a consistent pool of potential tenants or buyers, supporting sustained demand.

- **Consumer Spending and Retail Activity:** Consumer spending patterns and retail activity reflect the purchasing power and lifestyle dynamics of a market. Vibrant retail sectors and robust consumer spending are indicative of economic prosperity.

- **Interest Rates and Financing Accessibility:** The accessibility of financing and prevailing interest rates impact the affordability of real estate. Low-interest rates and favorable financing conditions contribute to increased demand, while high-interest rates may have the opposite effect.

In conclusion, market research serves as the compass guiding real estate investors towards profitable opportunities. Techniques for identifying potential profitability, such as assessing supply and demand dynamics, analyzing economic indicators, and staying attuned to emerging trends, empower investors to make informed decisions. Additionally, delving into demographics and economic trends provides a nuanced understanding of market viability, allowing investors to align their strategies with the dynamic needs of specific populations. By navigating the intricate landscape of market research, real estate investors position themselves for success in an ever-evolving industry.

Section 2: Understanding Buyer and Seller Behavior - Navigating the Psychology of Real Estate Transactions

Real estate transactions are not just transactions; they are complex interactions influenced by a myriad of psychological factors. In this section, we will delve into the intricacies of understanding buyer and seller behavior, exploring the psychographics of real estate clients and dissecting the factors that influence their buying and selling decisions.

A. Psychographics of Real Estate Clients: Deciphering the Psychological Factors

1. Understanding the Psychological Factors Influencing Client Decisions

Real estate decisions are deeply influenced by psychological factors that go beyond mere property specifications. Understanding these factors allows real estate investors to connect with clients on a deeper level and tailor their services to meet both rational and emotional needs.

- **Emotional Triggers:** Real estate transactions are inherently emotional. Whether it's the excitement of buying a dream home or the nostalgia associated with selling a property, emotional triggers play a significant role. Understanding and empathizing with these emotions builds trust and rapport.

- **Lifestyle Preferences:** Clients' lifestyles and preferences are integral to their real estate choices. Factors such as proximity to amenities, preferred neighborhood vibes, and desired community attributes shape their decisions. Tailoring property suggestions to align with these preferences enhances client satisfaction.

- **Risk Tolerance:** Real estate is an investment fraught with perceived risks. Understanding clients' risk tolerance levels helps in presenting suitable investment options. Some clients may prioritize stable, long-term investments, while others might seek higher-risk, high-reward opportunities.

- **Future Aspirations:** Buyer and seller decisions are often influenced by their future aspirations. A growing family might seek a larger home, while empty nesters may look to downsize. Aligning real estate offerings with clients' future aspirations ensures long-term satisfaction.

2. Creating Buyer Personas for Targeted Marketing

Buyer personas are detailed representations of ideal clients based on demographic, psychographic, and behavioral characteristics. Developing these personas helps in crafting targeted marketing strategies that resonate with specific client segments.

- **Demographic Information:** Define buyer personas by considering demographic factors such as age, income, occupation, and family status. These details form the foundational understanding of who the ideal clients are.

- **Psychographic Insights:** Dive into psychographic insights by exploring clients' interests, hobbies, values, and lifestyle choices. Understanding the psychographics helps in tailoring marketing messages that appeal to clients on a personal level.

- **Communication Preferences:** Buyer personas should encompass communication preferences. Some clients may prefer in-person meetings, while others favor digital communication. Adapting communication styles to match buyer personas enhances engagement.

- **Challenges and Pain Points:** Identify the challenges and pain points of different buyer personas. Whether it's navigating the complexities of the buying process or concerns about property resale, addressing these challenges proactively strengthens client relationships.

- **Tailoring Marketing Content:** Craft marketing content that speaks directly to the identified buyer personas. Whether it's social media campaigns, blog posts, or property listings, tailoring content ensures relevance and resonance.

B. Factors Influencing Buying and Selling Decisions: The Intersection of Emotion and Rationality

1. Explore the Emotional and Rational Aspects of Decision-Making

Real estate transactions are a delicate balance between emotion and rationality. Recognizing and navigating this intersection is essential for real estate investors seeking to align their marketing strategies with the motivations of buyers and sellers.

- **Emotional Aspects:** Emotional aspects heavily influence buying and selling decisions. The joy of homeownership, the satisfaction of finding the perfect property, or the emotional ties to a family home all contribute to the decision-making process. Acknowledging and addressing these emotions builds trust.

- **Rational Considerations:** While emotions drive decisions, rational considerations also play a pivotal role. Factors such as property value, investment potential, and future resale value are critical rational elements that clients weigh in their decision-making process.

- **Risk Mitigation:** Real estate transactions involve perceived risks. Clients want assurance that their investments are sound and that potential risks are mitigated. Providing transparent information, market analyses, and risk assessments helps alleviate concerns.

- **Market Conditions and Timing:** Rational decisions often hinge on market conditions and timing. Buyers may strategically time purchases to capitalize on market trends, while sellers may assess optimal times for listing properties to maximize returns.

2. Strategies for Aligning Marketing with Buyer and Seller Motivations

Understanding the motivations behind buyer and seller decisions allows real estate investors to tailor their marketing strategies effectively. Aligning marketing efforts with these motivations creates resonance and enhances the overall client experience.

- **Crafting Compelling Narratives:** Develop marketing narratives that resonate with clients' motivations. Whether it's highlighting the potential for creating lasting memories in a new home or emphasizing the investment potential of a property, crafting compelling stories engages clients emotionally.

- **Educational Content for Informed Decisions:** Empower clients to make informed decisions by providing educational content. This could include market trend reports, guides on navigating the buying or selling process, and insights into potential risks and rewards.

- **Personalized Recommendations:** Tailor property recommendations based on clients' motivations. If a buyer is motivated by a desire for a peaceful suburban lifestyle, focus on properties in serene neighborhoods. For sellers motivated by maximizing returns, provide strategies for property enhancement and staging.

- **Transparent Communication:** Transparent communication builds trust by addressing both emotional and rational aspects. Communicate openly about market conditions, potential challenges, and the reasoning behind specific recommendations. Clients appreciate transparency in the decision-making process.

- **Flexible Marketing Strategies:** Recognize that buyer and seller motivations vary. Implement flexible marketing strategies that can be adjusted to align with different client motivations. A one-size-fits-all approach may not resonate with diverse client needs.

In conclusion, understanding the intricacies of buyer and seller behavior in real estate involves delving into the psychological factors that influence decisions. By grasping the emotional triggers, lifestyle preferences, and future aspirations of clients, real estate investors can create targeted marketing strategies that resonate on a personal level. Additionally, recognizing the intersection of emotion and rationality in decision-making allows professionals to align their marketing efforts with the motivations of buyers and sellers, fostering trust and long-term satisfaction. Crafting buyer personas, tailoring content, and providing transparent communication form the pillars of a successful approach to navigating the psychology of real estate transactions.

Section 3: Niche Marketing - Precision in the Diversity of Real Estate

In the vast landscape of real estate, finding success often involves more than a broad-strokes approach. Niche marketing is the art of identifying specialized markets within the industry and tailoring strategies to meet the unique needs of these segments. In this section, we'll explore the nuances of niche marketing, from identifying and capitalizing on specialized markets to crafting tailored strategies for specific niches.

A. Identifying and Capitalizing on Specialized Markets: Unlocking Niche Opportunities

1. Identifying Niche Markets Within the Real Estate Industry

Niche markets represent specific segments within the broader real estate landscape. Recognizing and understanding these niches is essential for real estate investors seeking to leverage targeted strategies.

- **Demographic-Based Niches:** Demographic-based niches cater to specific population segments with unique preferences and needs. Examples include senior housing, student housing, or properties designed for single professionals.

- **Geographic Niches:** Geographic niches focus on properties within specific locations or neighborhoods. This could involve specializing in luxury properties in a particular city, waterfront homes, or suburban communities.

- **Property Type Niches:** Specializing in specific property types, such as condominiums, vacation rentals, or commercial properties, allows real estate investors to become experts in those niches.

- **Lifestyle-Based Niches:** Lifestyle-based niches revolve around the preferences and lifestyles of target audiences. This could include eco-friendly or sustainable properties, smart homes, or properties tailored for specific hobbies or interests.

- **Investor-Focused Niches:** Catering to the unique needs of real estate investors forms another niche. This could involve targeting fix-and-flip investors, those interested in rental properties, or individuals seeking properties for short-term vacation rentals.

2. Tailoring Marketing Strategies to Meet the Unique Needs of

Niche Markets

Once niche markets are identified, tailoring marketing strategies to meet the unique needs of these segments becomes paramount. Precision in messaging and approach is key to resonating with niche audiences.

- **In-Depth Market Research:** Conduct comprehensive market research specific to the identified niche. Understand the preferences, pain points, and decision-making factors unique to that market segment.

- **Personalized Messaging and Content:** Craft messaging and content that speaks directly to the needs and aspirations of the niche audience. Whether it's emphasizing energy-efficient features, proximity to specific amenities, or investment potential, personalization is crucial.

- **Specialized Advertising Channels:** Utilize advertising channels that are most effective for the identified niche. This could involve targeted online advertising, industry-specific publications, or partnerships with platforms catering to that niche.

- **Networking Within the Niche Community:** Build relationships within the niche community. Attend events, engage with local groups, and become a recognized expert within that specific market segment.

- **Customized Services and Offerings:** Tailor services to match the unique needs of the niche market. This could involve offering specialized property tours, creating custom marketing materials, or providing insights specific to that niche.

B. Tailoring Marketing Strategies for Specific Niches: Crafting Messages for Success

1. Crafting Messages and Campaigns that Resonate with Specific Niche Audiences

The success of niche marketing hinges on the ability to craft messages and campaigns that resonate with the specific needs and desires of the target niche audience.

- **Understanding Niche Pain Points:** Identify the pain points within the niche market. Whether it's the need for accessible housing options for seniors or the desire for eco-friendly features, understanding these pain points informs the messaging strategy.

- **Highlighting Unique Selling Propositions:** Clearly communicate the unique selling propositions (USP) of properties within the niche. This could involve showcasing specific features, amenities, or investment benefits that set these properties apart.

- **Emphasizing Lifestyle Benefits:** Lifestyle-based niches often revolve around specific lifestyles or preferences. Craft messages that emphasize how the properties cater to and enhance the desired lifestyle of the niche audience.

- **Utilizing Visual Storytelling:** Visual storytelling is a powerful tool in niche marketing. Use images, videos, and virtual tours to convey the unique aspects of properties within the niche. Visuals create a compelling narrative that resonates with the target audience.

2. Examples of Successful Niche Marketing in Real Estate: Learning from the Pioneers

Examining real-world examples of successful niche marketing in real estate provides valuable insights into the strategies employed by industry pioneers.

- **Senior Housing Communities:** Real estate developers specializing in senior housing have successfully marketed their communities by focusing on factors like accessibility, safety features, and a sense of community. Messaging often emphasizes a worry-free, vibrant lifestyle tailored to seniors.

- **Eco-Friendly Properties:** Developers and real estate agents promoting eco-friendly properties highlight sustainable features such as solar panels, energy-efficient appliances, and green building materials. Marketing strategies focus on the environmental benefits and potential cost savings for environmentally conscious buyers.

- **Luxury Waterfront Homes:** Marketing luxury waterfront homes involves emphasizing exclusive features like panoramic views, private docks, and high-end amenities. Visual storytelling through high-quality images and videos creates an aspirational narrative for potential buyers seeking a premium lifestyle.

- **Investment-Focused Properties:** Real estate investors catering to investors often craft campaigns highlighting potential return on investment, market trends, and strategies for successful property management. Educational content and data-driven insights appeal to investors seeking profitable opportunities.

- **Vacation Rental Properties:** Marketing vacation rental properties involves showcasing unique features, proximity to attractions, and the potential for rental income. Targeted campaigns often focus on the experiential aspects of owning a vacation property.

In conclusion, niche marketing in real estate is a strategic approach that involves identifying and capitalizing on specialized markets. Whether targeting specific demographics, geographic locations, property types, lifestyle preferences, or investor needs, the precision in understanding and catering to niche audiences can lead to significant success. Tailoring marketing strategies, crafting personalized messages, and learning from examples of successful niche marketing pioneers empower real estate investors to navigate the diverse landscape of the industry with precision and accuracy.

Section 4: Competitive Analysis - Navigating Real Estate's Competitive Landscape

In the dynamic realm of real estate, understanding and navigating the competitive landscape is integral to success. This section explores the art of competitive analysis, from identifying and assessing competitors in target markets to differentiating offerings through strategic branding and marketing.

A. Analyzing Competitors in Your Target Markets: Unveiling the Playing Field

1. Methods for Identifying and Assessing Competitors

Before embarking on a strategic journey, real estate investors must first understand who they are up against in their target markets. Identifying and assessing competitors involves systematic methods to unveil the playing field.

- **Market Research and Surveys:** Conduct thorough market research to identify competitors. Surveys and interviews with local residents, real estate investors, and industry experts provide insights into the key players in the market.

- **Online Presence and Reviews:** Explore the online presence of competitors. Analyze their websites, social media profiles, and online reviews. This not only identifies competitors but also provides insights into their strengths and weaknesses.

- **Networking and Industry Events:** Engage in networking within the industry. Attend real estate conferences, seminars, and local events. Networking provides firsthand information about competitors, their strategies, and their standing in the market.

- **Local Partnerships and Alliances:** Establish partnerships and alliances with local businesses. Collaborating with other professionals in the area provides opportunities to gain insights into their operations and client base.

- **Property Listings and Transactions:** Monitor property listings and transactions in the target market. Identify which agents or agencies are frequently involved in transactions. This on-the-ground observation helps in understanding the active players.

2. Tools and Techniques for Conducting a Thorough Competitive Analysis

Armed with knowledge about competitors, real estate investors can employ tools and techniques to conduct a thorough analysis. This involves dissecting various aspects of competitors' operations.

- **SWOT Analysis:** Perform a SWOT (Strengths, Weaknesses, Opportunities, Threats) analysis for each identified competitor. This structured approach provides a comprehensive understanding of internal and external factors influencing competitors.

- **Comparative Market Analysis (CMA):** Conduct a comparative market analysis on a few properties to assess how competitors price their properties. Analyzing pricing strategies provides insights into market trends and helps in positioning offerings competitively.

- **Digital Analytics Tools:** Utilize digital analytics tools to assess online performance. Tools like Google Analytics, social media analytics, and website traffic analysis reveal how competitors attract and engage their online audience.

- **Customer Feedback and Testimonials:** Scrutinize customer feedback and testimonials for competitors. Analyzing what clients appreciate or criticize about competitors' services informs areas for differentiation.

- **Regulatory Compliance and Reputation:** Ensure competitors are compliant with local regulations and ethical standards. A solid reputation built on adherence to rules and ethical practices contributes to long-term success.

B Differentiating Your Offerings: Strategies for Standing Out in a Crowded Field

1. Strategies for Highlighting Unique Selling Propositions

With a comprehensive understanding of competitors, the next step is to differentiate offerings by highlighting unique selling propositions (USPs). This involves identifying what sets a real estate professional apart and leveraging those differentiators.

- **Specialized Expertise:** Showcase specialized expertise in a particular niche or property type. Whether it's luxury homes, commercial properties, or sustainable housing, positioning as an expert in a specific field creates a competitive advantage.

- **Exceptional Customer Service:** Prioritize exceptional customer service as a USP. Providing personalized attention, transparent communication, and going above and beyond for clients differentiate a real estate professional in the eyes of customers.

- **Innovative Marketing Strategies:** Innovate in marketing strategies. Embrace new and creative approaches that stand out in a crowded market. This could involve interactive virtual tours, engaging social media campaigns, or unique property presentations.

- **Technology Integration:** Leverage technology to enhance the client experience. Whether it's utilizing virtual reality for property tours, implementing advanced CRM systems, or adopting cutting-edge communication tools, integrating technology demonstrates a commitment to modern and efficient practices.

2. Creating a Competitive Advantage through Branding and Marketing

As mentioned in the previous section on branding, branding and marketing play pivotal roles in creating a *competitive advantage*. A strong and distinctive brand, coupled with effective marketing strategies, positions a real estate professional as the go-to choice in the market.

- **Developing a Strong Brand Identity:** Invest in developing a strong brand identity. This involves crafting a memorable logo, defining brand values, and creating a consistent visual language across all marketing materials.

- **Crafting Compelling Brand Messaging:** Develop compelling brand messaging that resonates with the target audience. Clearly communicate what sets the brand apart and why clients should choose a particular real estate professional over competitors.

Competitive analysis is not just about understanding rivals but leveraging that understanding to carve out your unique space in the market. By consistently assessing competitors, utilizing effective tools, and crafting a distinctive brand, real estate investors can navigate competition successfully.

Section 5: Data-Driven Decision Making - The Power of Precision in Real Estate Marketing

In the ever-evolving landscape of real estate, the ability to make informed decisions is a cornerstone of success. This section delves into the realm of data-driven decision-making, exploring the integral role of data in refining marketing strategies and providing practical insights into implementing analytics tools for real estate marketing.

A. Utilizing Data for Informed Marketing Decisions: The Catalyst for Precision

1. The Role of Data in Refining Marketing Strategies

In an era where information is abundant, harnessing the power of data is essential for real estate investors looking to refine their marketing strategies. Data serves as a compass, guiding decision-making processes with precision.

- **Understanding Customer Behavior:** Data analytics allows real estate investors to delve into customer behavior. From understanding the properties clients frequently view to identifying preferred communication channels, this data forms the foundation for targeted and effective marketing.

- **Optimizing Channel Effectiveness:** Different marketing channels yield varying results. By analyzing data on engagement, conversion rates, and audience demographics across different channels, professionals can optimize their strategies to focus on the most effective avenues.

- **Refining Target Audience Profiles:** Data aids in the creation and refinement of target audience profiles. By analyzing the characteristics and preferences of past clients, real estate investors can tailor marketing messages to resonate with specific segments, enhancing overall effectiveness.

- **Adapting to Market Trends:** Real estate markets are dynamic, influenced by trends that evolve over time. Data provides insights into market trends, allowing professionals to adapt their marketing strategies to align with the current demands and preferences of potential clients.

2. Incorporating Market Insights into Decision-Making Processes

Data-driven decision-making involves seamlessly integrating market insights into every step of the decision-making process. This not only enhances the relevance of marketing efforts but also positions professionals as adaptable and responsive to the market's pulse.

- **Real-Time Decision Adjustments:** In a fast-paced industry, the ability to make real-time adjustments is invaluable. Data analytics enables real estate investors to monitor ongoing campaigns, assess their impact, and make immediate adjustments to optimize performance.

- **Evaluating Campaign Effectiveness:** Post-campaign analysis is a critical aspect of data-driven decision-making. By evaluating the effectiveness of marketing campaigns through metrics such as conversion rates, lead generation, and client acquisition costs, professionals can gauge their return on investment and refine future strategies.

- **Predictive Modeling for Future Planning:** Utilizing predictive modeling based on historical data allows professionals to forecast future trends and client behaviors. This forward-looking approach aids in strategic planning, helping real estate investors stay ahead of market shifts.

- **Customer Segmentation for Personalization:** Data segmentation enables personalized marketing approaches. By categorizing clients based on their preferences, behaviors, and demographics, professionals can tailor messages and offerings to meet the unique needs of different segments, fostering stronger connections.

B. Implementing Analytics Tools: Enhancing Precision in Real Estate Marketing

1. Introduction to Analytics Tools for Real Estate Marketing

The implementation of analytics tools is the gateway to unlocking the full potential of data-driven decision-making in real estate marketing. These tools provide the necessary infrastructure to collect, analyze, and derive actionable insights from data.

- **Customer Relationship Management (CRM) Systems:** CRM systems serve as central hubs for organizing and analyzing customer data. They track interactions, manage client relationships, and provide valuable insights into client preferences, allowing for more personalized marketing strategies.

- **Website Analytics Platforms:** Tools such as Google Analytics offer a comprehensive view of website performance. From tracking user behavior to assessing the effectiveness of landing pages, website analytics empower professionals to optimize their online presence.

- **Social Media Insights:** Each social media platform provides its own set of analytics tools. Professionals can track engagement, audience demographics, and the performance of individual posts. Leveraging these insights enhances the effectiveness of social media marketing strategies.

- **Email Marketing Analytics:** Email marketing platforms offer analytics on open rates, click-through rates, and subscriber behavior. These insights enable professionals to refine their email campaigns, delivering content that resonates with recipients.

2. Practical Tips for Using Data to Optimize Marketing Campaigns

Implementation is only the first step; using data effectively requires a strategic approach. Practical tips for optimizing marketing campaigns through data-driven insights are essential for translating information into actionable strategies.

- **Set Clear Objectives and Key Performance Indicators (KPIs):** Before launching any campaign, define clear objectives and KPIs. Knowing what success looks like allows for focused data collection and analysis, guiding decision-making toward specific goals.

- **Regularly Review and Update Customer Profiles:** Customer profiles should be dynamic, reflecting changes in behavior and preferences. Regularly review and update customer profiles based on new data, ensuring that marketing strategies remain aligned with the evolving needs of the target audience.

- **Utilize A/B Testing for Continuous Improvement:** A/B testing involves comparing two versions of a marketing element to determine which performs better. Whether testing email subject lines, website layouts, or advertising copy, A/B testing provides valuable insights for continuous improvement

- **Embrace Artificial Intelligence (AI) for Predictive Analysis:** AI applications can analyze vast datasets to identify patterns and predict future trends. Embracing AI for predictive analysis enhances strategic planning, allowing professionals to proactively adjust their marketing strategies based on anticipated market shifts.

- **Invest in Training and Skill Development:** Data-driven decision-making requires a certain level of proficiency in data analysis. Invest in training and skill development for marketing teams to ensure they can effectively interpret and leverage data insights.

In conclusion, the integration of data-driven decision-making into real estate marketing is a catalyst for precision and success. From understanding customer behavior to implementing analytics tools and continuously optimizing campaigns, real estate investors equipped with robust data insights can navigate the complexities of the industry with confidence and strategic finesse.

Chapter 4: Digital Marketing Strategies

Section 1: Online Advertising - Navigating the Digital Landscape in Real Estate Marketing

The digital era has reshaped the landscape of real estate marketing, with online advertising emerging as a powerful tool for reaching and engaging potential clients. This section provides a comprehensive exploration of online advertising in real estate, encompassing the implementation of effective paid advertising campaigns and delving into the nuances of platforms and targeting strategies.

A. Implementing Effective Paid Advertising Campaigns: A Strategic Approach

1. Overview of Paid Advertising Channels in Real Estate

The realm of paid advertising channels in real estate is diverse, offering a plethora of options to showcase properties, build brand awareness, and generate leads. Understanding the nuances of these channels is crucial for crafting effective campaigns.

- **Search Engine Advertising:** Leveraging search engine advertising, such as Google Ads, enables real estate investors to appear prominently in search results. This is particularly effective for targeting users actively searching for properties or related services.

- **Social Media Advertising:** Platforms like Facebook, Instagram, and LinkedIn provide robust opportunities for real estate advertising. Social media advertising allows for highly targeted campaigns based on demographics, interests, and online behaviors.

- **Display Advertising:** Display advertising involves visually appealing banner ads displayed on websites, apps, or social media platforms. These visually engaging ads can significantly boost brand visibility and attract potential clients.

- **Video Advertising:** Video advertising, whether on YouTube, social media, or other platforms, offers a dynamic way to showcase properties. Video content allows for immersive experiences, making it an impactful tool in real estate marketing.

- **Retargeting Campaigns:** Retargeting involves showing ads to users who have previously interacted with a website or specific content. This strategy keeps the brand in front of potential clients, reinforcing engagement and encouraging them to take further action.

2. Strategies for Optimizing Ad Spend and Maximizing ROI

While the range of paid advertising channels is extensive, the key lies in optimizing ad spend to achieve the maximum return on investment (ROI). Implementing strategies that ensure efficiency and effectiveness is paramount.

- **Define Clear Objectives:** Before launching any paid advertising campaign, define clear objectives. Whether the goal is to generate leads, increase brand awareness, or drive website traffic, clarity on objectives guides the entire campaign strategy.

- **Targeted Audience Segmentation:** Precise audience segmentation is a cornerstone of effective advertising. Identify and segment the target audience based on demographics, interests, and behaviors to tailor messages that resonate with specific groups.

- **Utilize Compelling Ad Creatives:** The visual and textual elements of an ad are critical in capturing attention. Invest in compelling ad creatives that highlight the unique selling points of properties, evoke emotions, and encourage engagement.

- **Leverage Ad Scheduling:** Timing plays a crucial role in the effectiveness of advertising. Utilize ad scheduling to display ads during peak hours or when the target audience is most likely to be online, optimizing the chances of engagement.

- **Continuous Monitoring and Optimization:** Real-time monitoring of campaign performance is essential. Regularly analyze key metrics such as click-through rates, conversion rates, and cost per acquisition. Use these insights to make data-driven adjustments and optimize ongoing campaigns.

B. Platforms and Targeting Strategies: Precision in Reaching the Right Audience

1. Examination of Advertising Platforms

The choice of advertising platforms significantly influences the reach and impact of real estate campaigns. Different platforms cater to distinct audience segments and offer varied features, requiring a tailored approach.

- **Google Ads:** Google Ads is a powerhouse for search engine advertising. Real estate investors can bid on keywords related to their properties, ensuring visibility when users actively search for relevant terms.

- **Facebook Ads:** Facebook's extensive user base and sophisticated targeting options make it an ideal platform for real estate advertising. Advertisers can target users based on demographics, interests, and behaviors, ensuring their ads reach a highly relevant audience.

- **Instagram Ads:** Given the visual nature of real estate, Instagram is a valuable platform for showcasing properties through visually appealing ads. Instagram Ads, integrated with Facebook's advertising platform, allows for seamless cross-promotion.

- **LinkedIn Ads:** LinkedIn is particularly effective for targeting a professional audience. Real estate investors seeking to connect with businesses, investors, or individuals in specific industries can leverage LinkedIn Ads for targeted outreach.

- **YouTube Advertising:** Video content is a compelling tool in real estate marketing, and YouTube provides a platform to showcase property tours, neighborhood highlights, and expert insights. YouTube Ads enable real estate investors to reach a vast audience through engaging video content.

2. Targeting Techniques for Reaching Specific Real Estate Audiences

The success of online advertising lies in the precision of targeting. Real estate investors can employ various techniques to ensure their ads reach the right audience, maximizing the impact of their campaigns.

- **Geographic Targeting:** Real estate is inherently location-specific. Geographic targeting allows advertisers to narrow down their audience based on specific regions, cities, or neighborhoods, ensuring that ads are relevant to potential clients in those locations.

- **Demographic Targeting:** Understanding the demographics of the target audience is crucial. Demographic targeting allows advertisers to tailor their messages based on factors such as age, gender, income level, and other demographic variables.

- **Interest-Based Targeting:** Leveraging users' interests is a powerful targeting strategy. Real estate investors can reach audiences interested in topics such as home improvement, real estate investment, or interior design, aligning their ads with the interests of potential clients.

- **Behavioral Targeting:** Analyzing online behaviors provides insights into user intent. Behavioral targeting allows advertisers to reach audiences based on their online activities, ensuring that ads are displayed to users with a demonstrated interest in real estate.

- **Retargeting Strategies:** Retargeting, or remarketing, involves showing ads to users who have previously interacted with a website or specific content. This technique keeps the brand in front of potential clients, reminding them of properties they've shown interest in.

In conclusion, online advertising in real estate is a dynamic landscape that offers vast opportunities for reaching and engaging potential clients. Implementing effective paid advertising campaigns and leveraging the right platforms and targeting strategies are essential components of a successful digital marketing strategy in the real estate industry. As technology continues to evolve, real estate investors equipped with a strategic and data-driven approach to online advertising will thrive in the competitive digital landscape.

Section 2: Content Marketing - Building Trust and Authority in Real Estate

In the digital age, content has become a cornerstone of marketing strategies, and in the realm of real estate, its significance is paramount. This section delves into the art and science of content marketing, exploring the creation of valuable content for real estate audiences and the diverse range of formats that resonate within the industry.

A. Creating Valuable Content for Your Audience: The

Pillars of Trust and Authority

1. The Importance of Content in Building Trust and Authority

In an industry where trust is paramount, content serves as the vehicle for establishing credibility and authority. Real estate investors who consistently provide valuable, informative, and engaging content position themselves as trusted advisors.

- **Establishing Expertise:** Content allows real estate investors to showcase their expertise. Whether through insightful articles, market analyses, or expert interviews, sharing industry knowledge positions professionals as authorities in their field.

- **Building Credibility:** Credibility is built over time through consistent, high-quality content. Buyers and sellers are more likely to trust professionals who demonstrate a deep understanding of the market, offer valuable insights, and provide transparent information.

- **Fostering Transparency:** Real estate transactions involve significant financial decisions. Transparent and informative content helps demystify the process for clients, fostering a sense of transparency and openness in the professional-client relationship.

- **Engaging with Your Audience:** Content is a two-way street. Engaging with the audience through comments, social media interactions, and feedback channels not only builds a sense of community but also enhances the credibility of real estate investors by showcasing their responsiveness.

2. Types of Content that Resonate with Real Estate Audiences

Real estate audiences have diverse interests and preferences, making it crucial to diversify content types. Tailoring content to resonate with specific audience segments ensures broader reach and engagement.

- **Educational Content:** Providing educational content is an effective way to address the informational needs of audiences. Topics could range from understanding the home-buying process to explaining market trends and offering insights into property financing.

- **Property Showcases:** Visual content showcasing properties is a staple in real estate marketing. High-quality images, virtual tours, and videos allow potential buyers to explore properties remotely, creating a compelling visual narrative that enhances engagement.

- **Market Trends and Insights:** Real estate is inherently tied to market dynamics. Regularly sharing insights into market trends, property values, and emerging opportunities demonstrates a keen understanding of the industry and positions professionals as market experts.

- **Expert Interviews and Features:** Collaborating with industry experts or featuring interviews with professionals in related fields adds depth and credibility to content. Expert perspectives provide valuable insights and enhance the overall quality of the content.

B. Blogging, Videos, and Other Content Formats: A Multifaceted Approach

1. Strategies for Maintaining an Engaging Real Estate Blog

A well-maintained blog is a versatile tool for real estate investors, offering a platform to share insights, market updates, and engage with the audience. Implementing effective strategies ensures the blog remains a valuable resource.

- **Consistent Posting Schedule:** Consistency is key in blogging. Establishing a regular posting schedule – whether weekly, bi-weekly, or monthly – keeps the audience engaged and establishes the blog as a reliable source of information.

- **Keyword Optimization for SEO:** Incorporating relevant keywords in blog content enhances search engine visibility. Understanding the keywords potential clients use when searching for real estate information allows professionals to align their blog content with user intent.

- **Addressing Frequently Asked Questions:** Blog content can address common queries and concerns. Creating articles that provide answers to frequently asked questions not only serves the audience but also positions the professional as a helpful resource.

- **Visual Appeal with Images and Infographics:** Visual elements enhance the appeal of blog posts. Incorporating high-quality images, infographics, and charts makes content visually engaging, facilitating better comprehension and retention of information.

2. Leveraging Video Content for Property Showcases and Educational Content

Video content has become increasingly popular in the real estate industry due to its ability to convey information in a dynamic and engaging manner. Leveraging videos expands the reach and impact of content marketing strategies.

- **Property Showcases and Virtual Tours:** Video property showcases provide a immersive experience for potential buyers. From virtual tours to professionally produced property videos, this format allows clients to explore homes from the comfort of their own space.

- **Educational Videos and Tutorials:** Educational videos complement written content by providing visual explanations. Tutorials on home-buying processes, investment strategies, or interior design tips cater to audiences who prefer visual learning.

- **Live Streaming and Interactive Sessions:** Live streaming offers real-time interaction with the audience. Hosting live Q&A sessions, property walkthroughs, or market updates fosters a sense of immediacy and connection with the audience.

- **Behind-the-Scenes Content:** Offering a glimpse behind the scenes humanizes the professional. Videos showcasing a day in the life, office culture, or project development add a personal touch, strengthening the relationship with the audience.

In conclusion, content marketing is a dynamic and essential component of real estate strategies. By creating valuable content that builds trust and authority, and leveraging a mix of blogging, videos, and other formats, real estate investors can effectively engage their audience, showcase expertise, and establish a strong online presence in a competitive market. As the digital landscape continues to evolve, embracing innovative content marketing strategies positions professionals for sustained success in the ever-changing real estate industry.

Section 3: Search Engine Optimization (SEO) - Elevating Your Online Visibility in Real Estate Marketing

In the vast digital landscape of real estate marketing, Search Engine Optimization (SEO) stands as a linchpin for enhancing online visibility and driving organic traffic. This section delves into the fundamental principles of SEO, elucidating its pivotal role in increasing online visibility. Additionally, it provides practical insights into the intricate art of keyword research and on-page optimization, essential components of a robust SEO strategy in the real estate domain.

A. Optimizing Your Online Presence for Search Engines: The Foundations of SEO

1. The Role of SEO in Increasing Online Visibility

SEO is the cornerstone of online visibility, shaping the way real estate investors are discovered by potential clients in the vast realm of the internet. Its role extends beyond merely securing a higher ranking on search engine results; it is about crafting a digital presence that aligns with user intent.

- **Building Credibility and Trust:** A high-ranking position on search engine results pages (SERPs) is often associated with credibility and trustworthiness. Users inherently trust websites that appear at the top of search results, positioning SEO as a conduit for building a trustworthy online brand.

- **Enhancing User Experience:** SEO is not solely about appeasing search engines; it is about optimizing the user experience. Websites that are easily navigable, load quickly, and provide valuable content are rewarded by search engines, fostering positive interactions with potential clients.

- **Establishing Authority in the Real Estate Niche:** By consistently producing relevant and informative content, real estate investors can position themselves as authorities in their niche. SEO plays a crucial role in amplifying this authority, ensuring that the content is not only valuable to users but also favored by search engines.

- **Driving Organic Traffic:** Organic traffic, derived from users actively searching for real estate-related queries, is a valuable asset for professionals in the industry. SEO is the mechanism through which this organic traffic is cultivated, leading to a more sustainable and cost-effective approach to online visibility.

2. Best Practices for On-Page and Off-Page Optimization

On-page and off-page optimization are the twin pillars of an effective SEO strategy. While on-page elements directly impact the content and structure of a website, off-page factors extend beyond the site itself, encompassing factors such as backlinks and social signals.

On-Page Optimization

- *Content Relevance and Quality:* The cornerstone of on-page optimization is the content itself. Ensuring that content is not only relevant to real estate but also of high quality is imperative. This includes informative articles, property descriptions, and any text present on the website.

- *Optimizing Meta Titles and Descriptions:* Crafting compelling meta titles and descriptions that accurately reflect the content is crucial for attracting user clicks from the SERPs. These snippets serve as the first impression users have of the content on a webpage.

User-Friendly URLs and Navigation: Simplifying URLs and ensuring easy navigation contribute to a positive user experience. Search engines favor websites that are user-friendly, as it aligns with their goal of delivering the best possible results to users.

- *Mobile Optimization:* With the increasing prevalence of mobile users, optimizing websites for mobile devices is no longer a choice but a necessity. Search engines prioritize mobile-friendly sites, making mobile optimization a key aspect of on-page SEO.

Off-Page Optimization

- *Building High-Quality Backlinks:* Backlinks, or links from other reputable websites to yours, are a significant off-page ranking factor. However, the emphasis is on quality over quantity. High-quality backlinks from authoritative sources carry more weight in search engine algorithms.

- *Social Media Signals:* While the direct impact of social media on SEO is debated, social signals can indirectly influence rankings. Active social media engagement, shares, and mentions contribute to the overall online presence and authority of a real estate professional.

- *Online Reviews and Reputation Management:* Online reviews play a role in establishing credibility and trust. Positive reviews contribute to a positive online reputation, potentially influencing both users and search engines.

- *Local SEO:* For real estate investors targeting specific geographical areas, local SEO is pivotal. Optimizing business listings, ensuring consistency in NAP (Name, Address, Phone) information, and obtaining positive local reviews contribute to local SEO efforts.

B. Keyword Research and On-Page Optimization: Crafting a Language That Speaks to Your Audience

1. Techniques for Identifying Relevant Keywords in Real Estate

Keywords are the language that connects users with the content they seek. Identifying the right keywords is fundamental to an effective SEO strategy. In the real estate realm, where users may employ diverse search queries, mastering keyword research is an art.

- **Understanding User Intent:** Keyword research should begin with an understanding of user intent. What are potential clients searching for? What questions do they seek answers to? By aligning content with user intent, real estate investors can cater to the needs of their target audience.

- **Long-Tail Keywords for Specificity:** Long-tail keywords, comprising longer and more specific phrases, often reflect the nuanced queries users make when looking for real estate information. Incorporating these long-tail keywords into content ensures relevance to niche topics.

- **Utilizing Localized Keywords:** For real estate investors targeting specific geographic locations, incorporating localized keywords is crucial. This not only aligns with local SEO efforts but also ensures that content is tailored to the specific needs and preferences of users in that area.

- **Competitor Analysis for Keyword Insights:** Analyzing the keywords that competitors are targeting provides valuable insights. It helps identify gaps in content coverage, uncover emerging trends, and refine keyword strategies to remain competitive in the online space.

2. Implementing On-Page Optimization Strategies for Search

Engines

Once the relevant keywords are identified, the next step is to seamlessly integrate them into the website's content. On-page optimization ensures that search engines can interpret and rank the content accurately.

- **Strategic Placement of Keywords:** Keywords should be strategically placed in key areas such as titles, headings, and throughout the content. However, it's essential to maintain a natural flow, ensuring that the content reads well for users and does not feel forced.

- **Optimizing Image Alt Text:** Real estate websites often include a plethora of images showcasing properties. Optimizing image alt text with relevant keywords not only enhances accessibility for users with visual impairments but also provides an additional layer of context for search engines.

- **Creating Engaging Meta Descriptions:** While meta descriptions may not directly impact rankings, they serve as the snippet users see on the SERPs. Crafting compelling meta descriptions that incorporate keywords encourages user clicks and engagement.

- **Internal Linking Structure:** Building a cohesive internal linking structure aids in the navigation of both users and search engine crawlers. Internal links should be strategically placed, directing users to relevant pages and helping search engines understand the hierarchy and relationships between different content.

- **Regular Content Updates and Maintenance:** The freshness and relevance of content are key factors in SEO. Regularly updating and maintaining content not only ensures accuracy but also signals to search engines that the website is active and continually providing value to users.

In conclusion, SEO serves as the compass guiding real estate investors through the digital landscape. By understanding the multifaceted role of SEO in enhancing online visibility, optimizing on-page and off-page elements, and mastering the art of keyword research, real estate investors can navigate the intricacies of the digital realm with precision and purpose. As technology evolves and search engine algorithms continue to refine, staying attuned to SEO best practices is paramount for those seeking sustained success in real estate marketing.

Section 4: Email Marketing - Cultivating Relationships and Driving Engagement in Real Estate

In the dynamic realm of real estate marketing, where personalized communication and relationship-building are paramount, email marketing emerges as a potent tool. This section explores the intricacies of *email marketing*, unraveling the art of building and nurturing email lists. Additionally, it delves into the craft of crafting effective email campaigns, exploring best practices, automation, and drip campaigns for optimal lead nurturing.

A. Building and Nurturing Email Lists: Strategies for Sustainable Growth

1. Strategies for Growing a Targeted Email Subscriber Base

The foundation of effective email marketing lies in the quality and relevance of the email subscriber base. Building a targeted list ensures that communications resonate with recipients, fostering engagement and conversions.

- **Utilizing Lead Magnets:** Lead magnets are incentives offered to potential subscribers in exchange for their email addresses. In the real estate context, lead magnets can include resources such as property guides, market reports, or exclusive insights, enticing users to join the email list.

- **Leveraging Website Opt-in Forms:** Strategically placed opt-in forms on a real estate website provide users with the opportunity to subscribe to email updates. These forms should be user-friendly, clearly conveying the value of subscribing and aligning with the overall user experience.

- **Collaborating with Real Estate Partners:** Collaborating with other professionals in the real estate ecosystem, such as mortgage brokers, home inspectors, or interior designers, provides opportunities for cross-promotion. Partnering to offer joint resources or exclusive content can attract a wider audience to the email list.

- **Hosting Webinars and Virtual Events:** Webinars and virtual events offer an interactive platform for engagement. By requiring registration, real estate investors can collect email addresses from attendees, simultaneously providing valuable information and growing the subscriber base.

2. Importance of Segmentation for Personalized Communication

The era of one-size-fits-all communication is long gone. Segmentation is the key to delivering personalized and relevant content to different segments of the email list, enhancing engagement and ensuring that recipients receive information tailored to their interests.

- **Demographic Segmentation:** Segmenting the email list based on demographics such as age, location, or income level enables real estate investors to customize messages that resonate with specific groups. This ensures that content is not only relevant but also speaks directly to the unique needs of each segment.

- **Behavioral Segmentation:** Analyzing user behavior, such as engagement with previous emails or interactions on the website, provides insights into individual preferences. Behavioral segmentation allows for targeted communication, delivering content that aligns with the recipient's past interactions.

- **Stage of the Buyer's Journey:** Different stages of the buyer's journey warrant distinct types of communication. Segmenting the email list based on where individuals are in the buying process allows for the delivery of content that guides them seamlessly through each stage.

- **Preferences and Interests:** Gathering information about subscribers' preferences and interests enables real estate investors to tailor content accordingly. Whether it's specific property types, investment strategies, or neighborhood preferences, understanding individual interests enhances the relevance of communication.

B. Crafting Effective Email Campaigns: Best Practices in the Real Estate Industry

1. Email Campaign Best Practices in the Real Estate Industry

Crafting effective email campaigns requires a strategic approach that aligns with the nuances of the real estate industry. From captivating subject lines to compelling content, every element plays a role in driving engagement and achieving campaign objectives.

- **Compelling Subject Lines:** The subject line is the first impression and a decisive factor in whether an email gets opened. Compelling subject lines should be concise, intriguing, and relevant to entice recipients to open the email and explore its content.

- **Engaging Visual Content:** Real estate is inherently visual, and email campaigns should leverage this by incorporating engaging visual content. High-quality images, property tours, or interactive elements can capture the attention of recipients and convey information more effectively than text alone.

- **Clear Call-to-Action (CTA):** Every email should have a clear and actionable purpose. Whether it's prompting recipients to view a property, download a resource, or schedule a consultation, a well-defined call-to-action guides users towards the desired action.

- **Mobile-Friendly Design:** With a significant portion of email opens occurring on mobile devices, ensuring that email campaigns are optimized for mobile is essential. Responsive design and concise content enhance the user experience on various devices.

- **Personalization and Dynamic Content:** Personalizing emails based on recipient data, such as their name or previous interactions, creates a sense of individualized communication. Dynamic content that adapts based on user preferences or behaviors further enhances personalization.

2. Automation and Drip Campaigns for Lead Nurturing

Automation is a game-changer in email marketing, allowing real estate investors to nurture leads systematically and provide timely, relevant information throughout the buyer's journey using a software called an auto-responder.

- **Welcome Series:** A welcome series is an automated sequence of emails triggered when a user subscribes. It introduces new subscribers to the brand, sets expectations, and delivers valuable content, laying the foundation for a positive ongoing relationship.

- **Lead Nurturing Drip Campaigns:** Drip campaigns involve sending a series of pre-scheduled emails based on user actions or predefined time intervals. In real estate, lead nurturing drip campaigns can guide potential buyers through the decision-making process, providing insights, property information, and educational content.

- **Behavior-Based Automation:** Automation can be triggered based on specific user behaviors, such as clicking on certain links or engaging with particular content. Behavior-based automation ensures that subsequent emails align with the recipient's demonstrated interests.

- **Re-Engagement Campaigns:** Re-engagement campaigns target subscribers who have become inactive or disengaged. By sending targeted content or incentives, real estate investors can rekindle interest and encourage renewed engagement.

In conclusion, email marketing in real estate is not just about sending messages; it's about cultivating relationships, providing value, and guiding individuals through their real estate journey. By employing strategies for growing a targeted email list, understanding the significance of segmentation, and crafting effective campaigns with best practices and automation, real estate investors can leverage email as a powerful tool for engagement and conversion. In an industry where trust and personalized communication are paramount, mastering the art of email marketing is a pathway to sustained success.

Section 5: Social Media Marketing - Building Connections and Fostering Engagement in Real Estate

In the digital age, social media has become an indispensable tool for real estate investors seeking to connect with their audience, showcase properties, and build a dynamic online presence. This section delves into the nuances of social media marketing in the real estate realm, exploring the landscape of various platforms and providing insights into effective engagement strategies that foster community-building and maintain an active online presence.

A. Leveraging Social Platforms for Real Estate: A Multifaceted Approach

1. Overview of Social Media Platforms Suitable for Real Estate

The diverse landscape of social media platforms offers real estate investors a plethora of opportunities to connect with potential clients, showcase properties, and amplify their brand presence. Understanding the strengths and demographics of each platform is essential for tailoring content to the right audience.

- **Facebook:** As the largest social media platform, Facebook provides a broad reach and diverse audience. Real estate investors can utilize Facebook for property listings, virtual tours, and engaging content. The platform's advertising capabilities enable targeted campaigns to specific demographics and geographic areas.

- **Instagram:** A visual-centric platform, Instagram is ideal for showcasing visually appealing property images, videos, and stories. Features like IGTV allow for longer-form content, such as property tours or behind-the-scenes glimpses. Hashtags and location tags enhance discoverability within specific niches or geographic areas.

- **LinkedIn:** LinkedIn caters to a more professional audience, making it conducive for networking, B2B connections, and thought leadership. Real estate investors can share industry insights, engage in discussions, and connect with potential partners or clients.

- **Twitter:** Twitter's fast-paced nature is well-suited for real-time updates, industry news, and quick engagement. Real estate investors can participate in relevant conversations, share market trends, and amplify their reach through retweets and hashtags.

- **YouTube:** As a video-centric platform, YouTube is an excellent space for real estate investors to host property tours, educational content, and client testimonials. Optimizing video content for searchability enhances visibility within the platform and search engine results.

- **Pinterest:** Pinterest's visual discovery format is valuable for showcasing property aesthetics, interior design ideas, and neighborhood highlights. Real estate investors can create boards that resonate with specific buyer interests, contributing to a visually compelling online presence.

2. Tailoring Content for Different Social Media Channels

While a cohesive brand identity should permeate all social media channels, tailoring content to each platform's unique characteristics is crucial for optimal engagement.

- **Visual Appeal for Instagram and Pinterest:** Instagram and Pinterest thrive on visually appealing content. High-quality images, aesthetically pleasing property showcases, and curated boards can captivate the audience's attention. The use of Instagram Stories and Pinterest Pins adds a dynamic element to the visual narrative.

- **Professional Insights on LinkedIn:** LinkedIn's professional atmosphere calls for content that showcases expertise and thought leadership. Real estate investors can share market insights, industry trends, and professional achievements to position themselves as authoritative figures within the real estate landscape.

- **Conciseness and Hashtags on Twitter:** Twitter's character limit necessitates concise and impactful messaging. Real estate investors can leverage hashtags to join relevant conversations, amplify their tweets, and increase discoverability within the real estate community.

- **Interactive Videos on YouTube:** YouTube's video-centric format allows real estate investors to create engaging and informative content. Property tours, market updates, and educational videos can capture the audience's interest and keep them invested in the content.

B. Engaging with Your Audience: Strategies for Sustainable Interaction

1. Strategies for Fostering Engagement and Interaction on Social Media

Building an engaged online community goes beyond posting content; it involves fostering meaningful interactions, responding to queries, and actively participating in conversations.

- **Prompt and Personalized Responses:** Responding promptly to comments, messages, and inquiries demonstrates attentiveness and a commitment to customer service. Personalized responses add a human touch, making the audience feel valued and acknowledged.

- **Interactive Content:** Interactive content, such as polls, quizzes, and Q&A sessions, invites audience participation. Real estate investors can use these features to gather insights, gauge preferences, and involve the audience in decision-making processes.

- **Showcasing Behind-the-Scenes:** Providing glimpses behind the scenes humanizes the brand and builds a connection with the audience. Behind-the-scenes content can include office life, property preparation, or team highlights, creating a more relatable image.

- **User-Generated Content:** Encouraging users to create and share content related to the brand, such as testimonials, property photos, or experiences, enhances authenticity. Real estate investors can showcase user-generated content, fostering a sense of community and trust.

2. Building a Community and Maintaining an Active Online Presence

Building a community on social media involves creating an environment where users feel connected, informed, and inspired. Consistency, authenticity, and a proactive approach contribute to maintaining an active online presence.

- **Consistent Posting Schedule:** Establishing a consistent posting schedule helps in maintaining visibility and keeping the audience engaged. Real estate investors can leverage scheduling tools to plan content in advance, ensuring a steady flow of updates.

- **Utilizing Stories and Highlights:** Features like Instagram Stories and Highlights allow real estate investors to showcase time-sensitive content, announcements, and curated collections. These ephemeral formats create a sense of urgency and exclusivity, encouraging regular audience engagement.

- **Hosting Live Sessions:** Live sessions on platforms like Instagram or Facebook provide real-time interaction with the audience. Real estate investors can host Q&A sessions, virtual property tours, or live events, fostering a sense of immediacy and authenticity.

- **Monitoring and Responding to Trends:** Staying attuned to industry trends, viral content, and relevant discussions enables real estate investors to join conversations and adapt content to resonate with the current zeitgeist. Trend-related content enhances relatability and relevance.

- **Collaborating with Influencers and Partners:** Collaborating with influencers or industry partners amplifies reach and introduces the brand to new audiences. Joint campaigns, takeovers, or collaborative content contribute to a diverse and engaging online presence.

In conclusion, social media marketing in real estate is not just about broadcasting messages but creating a vibrant and interactive community. By leveraging the strengths of each social media platform, tailoring content for specific audiences, and implementing strategies for sustained engagement, real estate investors can cultivate a robust online presence that resonates with their target audience. Building connections, fostering engagement, and maintaining an active social media presence are integral components of a comprehensive real estate marketing strategy in the digital age.

Chapter 5: Offline Marketing Strategies

Section 1: Direct Mail Campaigns - Crafting Tangible Connections and Measuring Impact

In an era dominated by digital marketing, direct mail campaigns stand out as a tangible and impactful strategy for reaching target audiences. This section explores the intricacies of designing and executing targeted mailings, emphasizing the importance of compelling materials and strategies for honing in on specific demographics and geographies. Additionally, it delves into the critical aspect of measuring the effectiveness of direct mail campaigns, offering insights into implementing tracking mechanisms, analyzing metrics, and adjusting future campaigns for optimal results.

A. Designing and Executing Targeted Mailings: Crafting Compelling Connections

1. Crafting Compelling Direct Mail Materials

Direct mail materials serve as a physical representation of a brand's message, making the design and content crucial for capturing the recipient's attention. Crafting compelling materials involves a strategic blend of creativity, relevance, and a clear call-to-action.

- **Visual Appeal and Brand Consistency:** Visual elements play a pivotal role in direct mail materials. The design should align with the brand's identity, incorporating consistent colors, logos, and imagery. Visual appeal enhances the likelihood of recipients engaging with the content.

- **Clear Messaging and Call-to-Action:** Clarity in messaging is paramount. Direct mail should convey a clear and concise message, emphasizing the benefits or value proposition. Including a compelling call-to-action guides recipients on the desired next steps, whether it's visiting a website, contacting the sender, or participating in an offer.

- **Personalization and Relevance:** Personalizing direct mail materials based on recipient data, such as their name, location, or previous interactions, adds a personalized touch. Tailoring content to the recipient's needs or interests enhances relevance, increasing the likelihood of a positive response.

- **Incorporating High-Quality Imagery:** High-quality images of properties, promotional offers, or relevant visuals elevate the overall presentation. Crisp and captivating imagery contributes to the professional appearance of the direct mail piece, making it more appealing to recipients.

2. Strategies for Targeting Specific Demographics and Geographies

The success of a direct mail campaign hinges on targeting the right audience. Strategies for identifying specific demographics and geographies ensure that the campaign reaches individuals who are more likely to be interested in the offerings.

- **Data Analysis and Segmentation:** Analyzing demographic data and segmenting the target audience based on factors such as age, income, or property preferences allows for more precise targeting. This segmentation ensures that direct mail materials resonate with the unique characteristics of each audience segment.

- **Geographic Targeting and Localized Campaigns:** Tailoring direct mail campaigns to specific geographic areas aligns with the localized nature of real estate. Whether targeting a neighborhood, city, or region, understanding the unique characteristics of the area enables real estate investors to craft messages that resonate with local interests and needs.

- **Utilizing Purchase History and Preferences:** For individuals who have interacted with the brand or made previous purchases, leveraging their purchase history and preferences enhances targeting accuracy. Direct mail materials can be customized based on their past interactions, increasing the likelihood of a positive response.

- **Incorporating Seasonal or Timely Messaging:** Aligning direct mail campaigns with seasonal or timely themes adds relevance. For example, sending materials related to property maintenance tips in the spring or showcasing holiday promotions demonstrates an understanding of the recipient's current needs and interests.

B. Measuring the Effectiveness of Direct Mail: Implementing Tracking Mechanisms

1. Implementing Tracking Mechanisms for Direct Mail Campaigns

Unlike some digital marketing channels, direct mail campaigns can be more challenging to track. However, implementing tracking mechanisms is essential for gauging effectiveness, understanding recipient behavior, and refining future campaigns.

- **Unique QR Codes or PURLs:** Incorporating unique QR codes or personalized URLs (PURLs) in direct mail materials enables easy tracking. Recipients can use their smartphones to scan QR codes or visit personalized web addresses, providing insights into who engaged with the content and what actions they took.

- **Customized Landing Pages:** Creating customized landing pages specifically for the direct mail campaign allows for more detailed tracking. The landing page can feature unique elements mentioned in the direct mail piece, and analytics tools can capture data on visitor behavior, conversions, and other relevant metrics.

- **Call Tracking Numbers:** Assigning specific phone numbers for direct mail campaigns facilitates tracking of incoming calls. Call tracking numbers, distinct from regular business lines, enable real estate investors to attribute phone inquiries directly to the direct mail initiative.

- **Coupon Codes and Promotional Offers:** Including exclusive coupon codes or promotional offers in direct mail materials encourages recipients to redeem them. By tracking the usage of these codes, real estate investors can measure the impact of the campaign and assess the effectiveness of specific incentives.

C. Analyzing Metrics and Adjusting Future Campaigns: Leveraging Insights for Optimization

1. Analyzing Metrics for Informed Decision-Making

The analysis of metrics goes beyond measuring the success or failure of a direct mail campaign; it provides valuable insights into recipient behavior, preferences, and areas for improvement.

- **Response Rates and Conversion Metrics:** Calculating response rates, including the number of inquiries or actions taken in response to the direct mail campaign, provides a foundational understanding of its impact. Conversion metrics, such as the number of leads generated or properties sold, offer insights into the ultimate success of the campaign.

- **Audience Segmentation Performance:** Assessing the performance of different audience segments allows real estate investors to identify which demographics or geographies responded most positively. This insight informs future targeting strategies and helps tailor content to resonate with specific segments.

- **Engagement with Personalized Elements:** If personalized elements, such as QR codes, PURLs, or customized landing pages, were incorporated, analyzing engagement with these elements provides insights into individual recipient interactions. This data sheds light on which personalized strategies were most effective.

- **Tracking Changes in Brand Recognition:** Direct mail campaigns contribute to brand recognition, and tracking changes in brand perception or recall can be indicative of the campaign's impact. Surveys or feedback mechanisms can gauge shifts in brand sentiment among the target audience.

2. Adjusting Future Campaigns Based on Insights

Armed with the insights gleaned from metrics analysis, real estate investors can make informed adjustments to optimize future direct mail campaigns.

- **Refining Targeting Parameters:** If certain demographic segments showed higher engagement, refining targeting parameters to focus more on these segments can enhance future campaign effectiveness. Data-driven adjustments ensure that resources are allocated where they yield the greatest impact.

- **Optimizing Design and Messaging:** Insights into recipient preferences and engagement patterns can inform optimizations in design and messaging. Testing variations in design elements, messaging styles, or calls-to-action allows for continual refinement based on real-world performance.

- **Exploring New Creatives and Formats:** Direct mail is a versatile medium, and experimenting with new creatives, formats, or innovative approaches can capture attention. Whether exploring augmented reality elements, interactive features, or unique packaging, staying open to creative evolution keeps campaigns fresh and engaging.

- **Iterative Testing and Continuous Improvement:** Adopting an iterative approach to testing and refining campaigns ensures continuous improvement. Real estate investors can implement small changes in each iteration, monitor their impact, and build upon successful elements over time.

In conclusion, direct mail campaigns offer a tangible and personalized avenue for real estate investors to connect with their audience. By investing in compelling design, targeting specific demographics and geographies strategically, implementing effective tracking mechanisms, and leveraging insights for future optimizations, direct mail becomes a dynamic and measurable component of a comprehensive real estate marketing strategy. Balancing creativity with data-driven decision-making ensures that direct mail campaigns not only resonate with recipients but also contribute to the overall success of the marketing endeavors in the competitive real estate landscape.

Section 2: Networking Events and Seminars - Cultivating Connections and Establishing Authority in Real Estate

Networking events and seminars are integral components of a robust real estate marketing strategy, offering unique opportunities to forge connections, exchange knowledge, and establish authority within the industry. This section explores the significance of industry events and strategies for effective hosting and participation. Additionally, it delves into the planning and execution of seminars as a powerful avenue for building authority, credibility, and fostering valuable relationships.

A. Hosting and Participating in Industry Events: The Power of Networking

1. The Significance of Industry Events in Real Estate

Industry events, whether conferences, trade shows, or local meet-ups, serve as crucial forums for real estate investors to connect with peers, potential clients, and industry influencers. The significance of these events lies in their ability to facilitate networking, knowledge sharing, and exposure to emerging trends.

- **Building a Network of Contacts:** Networking is the heartbeat of the real estate industry. Industry events provide a fertile ground to expand professional networks, fostering relationships that can lead to collaborative ventures, referrals, and valuable partnerships.

- **Exposure to Industry Trends and Innovations:** Staying abreast of industry trends is imperative for real estate investors. Industry events offer a concentrated environment where attendees can gain insights into the latest market trends, technological innovations, and best practices.

- **Opportunities for Collaboration and Partnerships:** Collaborative opportunities often emerge from industry events. Whether it's forming partnerships with other real estate investors, collaborating with service providers, or exploring joint ventures, the collaborative spirit of these events can open doors to new possibilities.

2. Strategies for Hosting and Participating Effectively

Maximizing the benefits of industry events requires thoughtful planning and strategic participation. Real estate investors can employ various strategies to make the most of these opportunities.

- **Pre-event Preparation and Research:** Before attending or hosting an industry event, thorough preparation is essential. Researching the event agenda, speakers, and attendees helps identify key individuals to connect with and ensures a targeted approach to networking.

- **Strategic Engagement During Events:** Actively engaging with attendees, participating in discussions, and attending relevant sessions contribute to a meaningful presence at industry events. Real estate investors should aim for quality interactions over quantity, focusing on building meaningful connections.

- **Utilizing Digital Platforms for Event Promotion:** In the digital age, leveraging online platforms to promote attendance or host virtual components of an event enhances visibility. Social media, email marketing, and event-specific platforms can be powerful tools for generating interest and participation.

- **Effective Follow-up After Events:** The value of networking extends beyond the event itself. Implementing a robust follow-up strategy, such as sending personalized emails, connecting on professional networking platforms, or scheduling post-event meetings, solidifies the relationships established during the event.

B. Establishing Authority Through Seminars: Building Credibility Through Education

1. Planning and Conducting Informative Seminars

Seminars provide real estate investors with a platform to share knowledge, expertise, and insights with their target audience. Planning and conducting informative seminars require a strategic approach to deliver valuable content and position the presenter as an authority in their field.

- **Identifying Relevant Topics and Themes:** The success of a seminar hinges on its relevance to the audience. Real estate investors should identify topics that align with the interests and concerns of their target audience, addressing pain points or providing solutions.

- **Choosing the Right Format and Delivery Method:** Seminars can take various formats, including in-person events, webinars, or workshops. The choice of format depends on the target audience, the nature of the content, and logistical considerations. The goal is to create an engaging and accessible learning experience.

- **Securing Engaging Speakers and Panelists:** Collaborating with knowledgeable and engaging speakers or panelists enhances the seminar's appeal. Industry experts, thought leaders, or professionals with unique insights can contribute to the overall value of the event.

- **Promoting Seminars Effectively:** Successful seminars require effective promotion to attract the intended audience. Leveraging marketing channels such as email campaigns, social media, and partnerships with industry organizations amplifies reach and ensures maximum attendance.

2. Building Authority and Credibility Through Educational Events

Seminars serve as a powerful tool for building authority and credibility within the real estate industry. By positioning themselves as educators and thought leaders, real estate investors can enhance their reputation and influence.

- **Demonstrating Expertise and Thought Leadership:** Through well-researched and insightful presentations, real estate investors can demonstrate their expertise and thought leadership. Sharing valuable insights, case studies, and actionable advice positions the presenter as a trusted source of information.

- **Q&A Sessions and Audience Interaction:** Incorporating interactive elements, such as Q&A sessions or audience polls, fosters engagement and allows participants to directly interact with the presenter. This interaction not only enhances the learning experience but also builds a connection between the presenter and the audience.

- **Providing Tangible Takeaways for Attendees:** Seminars should offer tangible takeaways for attendees, whether it's practical tips, actionable strategies, or exclusive resources. Providing value ensures that participants leave the event with valuable insights they can apply in their real estate endeavors.

- **Collecting and Showcasing Positive Feedback:** Positive feedback and testimonials from seminar attendees contribute to building credibility. Real estate investors can leverage these testimonials in future marketing efforts, showcasing the impact of their educational events.

In conclusion, networking events and seminars are dynamic elements of a comprehensive real estate marketing strategy, contributing to the cultivation of valuable connections and the establishment of authority within the industry. By strategically approaching industry events, fostering meaningful connections, and positioning themselves as educators and thought leaders through seminars, real estate investors can elevate their visibility, credibility, and influence in a competitive market. Balancing the art of networking with the science of education creates a synergistic approach that paves the way for long-term success in the dynamic realm of real estate.

Section 3: Traditional Advertising - Navigating the Landscape of Print and Broadcast Media in Real Estate

In the ever-evolving landscape of real estate marketing, traditional advertising methods continue to hold significance, especially through print and broadcast media. This section explores the role of traditional advertising in the real estate industry, examining how to craft impactful messages for print and broadcast channels. Additionally, it delves into the strategic interplay between traditional and digital advertising, highlighting the importance of creating cohesive campaigns that leverage the strengths of each medium.

A. Utilizing Print and Broadcast Media: The Enduring Power of Traditional Advertising

1. Assessing the Role of Traditional Advertising in Real Estate

Despite the rise of digital marketing, traditional advertising channels such as print and broadcast media retain a unique influence in the real estate industry. Understanding the role of traditional advertising involves recognizing its strengths and the specific contexts in which it excels.

- **Print Media's Tangible Appeal:** Print media, including newspapers, magazines, and direct mail, provides a tangible and lasting presence. In real estate, showcasing property listings, promotions, or brand messages through visually appealing print materials can capture the attention of a local audience.

- **Broadcast Media's Reach and Engagement:** Broadcast media, encompassing television and radio, offers broad reach and engagement. Television commercials can visually showcase properties, while radio ads convey messages to a diverse audience during their daily routines, making it a powerful tool for brand awareness.

- **Localized Impact in Specific Markets:** Traditional advertising allows for localized impact in specific markets. Regional newspapers, community magazines, and local radio stations enable real estate investors to tailor their messages to resonate with the unique characteristics of a particular area.

- **Building Trust and Credibility:** Traditional advertising, especially through established print publications or reputable broadcast channels, contributes to building trust and credibility. Consistent visibility in trusted media outlets reinforces the reliability and professionalism of a real estate brand.

2. Crafting Impactful Messages for Print and Broadcast Channels

Crafting messages for traditional advertising channels requires an understanding of the medium's strengths and the preferences of the target audience. Tailoring messages to resonate effectively ensures that the investment in traditional advertising yields the desired outcomes.

- **Visual Storytelling in Print:** Print media relies heavily on visual elements. Crafting impactful messages involves employing visual storytelling techniques, including high-quality images of properties, compelling headlines, and concise yet informative text that invites readers to engage further.

- **Emotional Appeal in Broadcast:** Broadcast media provides an opportunity to evoke emotions through audiovisual content. Crafting impactful messages for television or radio involves leveraging storytelling techniques that resonate emotionally with the audience, whether it's showcasing the charm of a neighborhood or highlighting the unique features of a property.

- **Highlighting Unique Selling Propositions:** In both print and broadcast advertising, emphasizing unique selling propositions (USPs) is crucial. Whether it's competitive pricing, exceptional service, or exclusive property features, clearly articulating what sets a real estate professional or property apart captures the audience's attention.

- **Call-to-Action for Audience Engagement:** Encouraging audience engagement is essential in traditional advertising. Including a clear call-to-action, whether it's visiting a website, contacting a real estate professional, or attending an open house, guides the audience on the next steps after encountering the advertisement.

B. Balancing Traditional and Digital Strategies: Creating Synergy for Maximum Impact

1. Strategies for Integrating Traditional and Digital Advertising

The most successful real estate marketing strategies recognize the symbiotic relationship between traditional and digital advertising. Integrating these strategies strategically ensures comprehensive coverage and engagement across a diverse audience.

- **Cross-Promotion Across Channels:** Cross-promotion involves reinforcing messages across both traditional and digital channels. For example, a print ad featuring a property can include a QR code or a specific website link, seamlessly connecting the audience to additional digital content for a more immersive experience.

- **Targeted Digital Campaigns Amplifying Traditional Messages:** Digital advertising allows for precise targeting based on demographics, interests, and online behavior. Combining traditional messages with targeted digital campaigns amplifies reach, ensuring that the key messages conveyed through print or broadcast are reinforced through digital touchpoints.

- **Social Media Amplification of Traditional Content:** Leveraging social media platforms to amplify traditional content extends its visibility. Real estate investors can share print materials or snippets from broadcast advertisements on social media, fostering engagement and reaching audiences who may not have encountered the traditional channels.

- **Data-Driven Insights Guiding Campaign Adjustments:** Both traditional and digital advertising generate valuable data. Integrating data-driven insights allows real estate investors to refine their campaigns continuously. Metrics such as engagement rates, click-through rates, and conversion data provide actionable information for adjusting strategies.

2. Creating Cohesive Campaigns Across Different Mediums

The synergy between traditional and digital advertising is most effective when campaigns are cohesive, presenting a unified brand image and messaging strategy. Creating synergy involves aligning visual elements, messaging, and overall branding across different mediums.

- **Consistent Branding and Visual Elements:** Consistency in branding elements, such as logos, color schemes, and typography, ensures a cohesive visual identity. Whether a potential client encounters a print ad, watches a television commercial, or visits a website, the consistent visual elements reinforce brand recognition.

- **Integrated Storytelling Across Channels:** Real estate marketing campaigns should tell a cohesive story across various channels. Whether it's the narrative of a property's unique features, the journey of a successful transaction, or the values that define a real estate professional, integrated storytelling creates a compelling and memorable experience for the audience.

- **Unified Call-to-Action Across Platforms:** A unified call-to-action (CTA) simplifies the audience's response. Whether the CTA is to schedule a viewing, explore more details on a website, or attend an event, presenting a consistent CTA across both traditional and digital channels streamlines the audience's engagement journey.

- **Monitoring and Adjusting in Real Time:** Real-time monitoring of campaign performance allows for immediate adjustments. Whether reallocating budget based on performance data, refining targeting parameters, or adapting messaging based on audience response, the ability to adjust in real time maximizes campaign effectiveness.

In conclusion, traditional advertising remains a potent force in real estate marketing, particularly through print and broadcast media. Crafting impactful messages for these channels involves understanding their unique strengths and tailoring content to resonate effectively. The strategic integration of traditional and digital advertising ensures comprehensive coverage, amplifies messaging, and leverages the strengths of each medium for maximum impact. By creating cohesive campaigns that present a unified brand image, real estate investors can harness the synergy of traditional and digital advertising to captivate their audience, build trust, and drive success in the dynamic real estate landscape. Balancing tradition with innovation paves the way for a holistic and effective marketing approach in the competitive realm of real estate.

Section 4: Local Partnerships - Nurturing Collaborative Alliances for Real Estate Marketing Success

In the dynamic landscape of real estate marketing, local partnerships emerge as powerful tools for building connections, enhancing community engagement, and expanding reach. This section explores the significance of building alliances with local businesses and delves into collaborative marketing strategies that mutually benefit both real estate investors and their local partners. Additionally, it provides examples of successful cross-promotions in real estate and outlines strategies for fostering meaningful collaborations.

A. Building Alliances with Local Businesses: The Cornerstone of Community-Centric Marketing

1. The Importance of Local Partnerships in Real Estate Marketing

Local partnerships form the bedrock of community-centric marketing strategies in real estate. Establishing connections with local businesses goes beyond transactional collaborations; it becomes a commitment to community building and fostering a positive and interconnected local ecosystem.

- **Enhancing Community Engagement:** Local partnerships contribute to enhanced community engagement. By aligning with businesses that share a geographical proximity, real estate investors can actively participate in the fabric of the community, gaining the trust and support of local residents.

- **Leveraging Local Expertise:** Collaborating with local businesses allows real estate investors to tap into the expertise and insights of those intimately familiar with the community. Whether it's understanding neighborhood dynamics, market trends, or local preferences, these collaborations offer valuable local intelligence.

- **Building a Trusted Network:** Local partnerships contribute to the creation of a trusted network. When real estate investors align themselves with reputable local businesses, they not only gain credibility through association but also foster a network of trusted allies who can vouch for their professionalism and commitment to the community.

2. Collaborative Marketing Strategies with Local Businesses

Successful collaborative marketing strategies with local businesses involve a thoughtful approach that aligns the goals and interests of both parties. From joint events to shared marketing campaigns, these strategies amplify the impact of marketing efforts and create a win-win scenario.

- **Coordinated Events and Sponsorships:** Hosting or sponsoring local events is a powerful way to collaborate with businesses. Real estate investors can partner with local restaurants, boutiques, or service providers to host community events, neighborhood clean-ups, or sponsor local sports teams, creating positive associations.

- **Joint Marketing Campaigns:** Collaborative marketing campaigns leverage the strengths of both the real estate professional and the local business. This could involve joint advertising efforts, co-branded promotional materials, or shared social media campaigns that highlight the symbiotic relationship between the two entities.

- **Exclusive Discounts and Offers:** Offering exclusive discounts or incentives in collaboration with local businesses adds value to the real estate professional's services. For example, partnering with a local furniture store to provide discounts for new homeowners creates a mutually beneficial arrangement that enhances the overall customer experience.

- **Community Outreach Programs:** Joint community outreach programs demonstrate a commitment to social responsibility. Real estate investors and local businesses can collaborate on initiatives such as charity drives, environmental projects, or educational programs, showcasing their dedication to making a positive impact on the community.

B. Cross-Promotions and Collaborations: Examples and Strategies for Success

1. Examples of Successful Cross-Promotions in Real Estate

Cross-promotions in real estate involve aligning with businesses whose products or services complement the real estate offering. Successful examples illustrate the diverse opportunities for collaboration within the real estate industry.

- **Realtor and Home Improvement Store Collaboration:** A realtor may collaborate with a local home improvement store to offer exclusive discounts on renovation materials for new homeowners. This not only benefits the new homeowners but also drives traffic to the home improvement store through the realtor's clientele.

- **Real Estate and Interior Design Partnership:** Collaborating with an interior design firm can enhance the appeal of a property. A real estate professional might offer a complimentary consultation with an interior designer for clients purchasing a new home, creating a seamless transition from property acquisition to personalized living spaces.

- **Property Developer and Local Restaurants Collaboration:** In a new residential development, a property developer might collaborate with local restaurants to provide residents with vouchers or discounts for dining. This enhances the lifestyle appeal of the neighborhood and supports local businesses.

- **Real Estate and Fitness Studio Partnership:** A real estate agent could partner with a local fitness studio to offer free or discounted memberships to new homeowners. This not only promotes a healthy lifestyle but also introduces new residents to local fitness amenities.

2. Strategies for Mutually Beneficial Collaborations

Fostering successful collaborations requires strategic planning, clear communication, and a commitment to creating value for all parties involved. Implementing these strategies enhances the likelihood of mutually beneficial and sustainable partnerships.

- **Identifying Complementary Businesses:** The foundation of a successful collaboration lies in identifying businesses that complement the real estate offering. Whether it's aligning with home service providers, local artisans, or lifestyle businesses, the synergy between the businesses enhances the overall customer experience.

- **Clear Communication and Goal Alignment:** Clear communication is paramount in any collaboration. Real estate investors and their local partners should align on goals, expectations, and the specific outcomes they aim to achieve through the collaboration. This ensures a unified approach and mitigates potential misunderstandings.

- **Creating Value for Both Audiences:** Successful collaborations create value for both audiences. The offerings or incentives provided through the collaboration should resonate with the shared interests of the audiences, ensuring that both the real estate professional and the local business receive positive responses from their respective customer bases.

- **Measuring and Adapting:** Implementing mechanisms for measuring the success of collaborations allows for continuous improvement. Metrics such as customer engagement, lead generation, or sales attributed to the collaboration provide insights into its effectiveness. Real-time monitoring enables both parties to adapt strategies for ongoing success.

In conclusion, local partnerships stand as a cornerstone for real estate investors seeking to create meaningful connections, enhance community engagement, and amplify their marketing impact. Building alliances with local businesses goes beyond transactional exchanges; it embodies a commitment to community building and a shared vision for the betterment of the local ecosystem. Collaborative marketing strategies, whether through coordinated events, joint campaigns, or exclusive offers, provide opportunities for real estate investors to create a positive and lasting impact on their communities.

Section 5: Community Engagement - Building Lasting Connections in Real Estate Marketing

In the realm of real estate marketing, community engagement emerges as a vital component for establishing lasting connections, fostering trust, and creating a positive brand image. This section explores the profound impact of community involvement and outlines strategies for real estate investors to actively participate in and contribute to local events. Additionally, it delves into the role of sponsorships and philanthropy, highlighting how these initiatives can be seamlessly incorporated into real estate marketing efforts.

A. Involvement in Community Events: The Power of Local Presence

1. The Impact of Community Involvement in Real Estate Marketing

Actively participating in community events provides real estate investors with a unique opportunity to establish a local presence and connect with residents on a personal level. The impact of such involvement extends beyond immediate marketing benefits, contributing to the overall fabric of community building.

- **Building Trust Through Presence:** Presence at local events builds trust. When real estate investors are actively involved in community gatherings, whether it's a neighborhood fair, charity run, or cultural celebration, they become familiar faces within the community. This familiarity enhances trust and credibility among residents.

- **Establishing a Positive Brand Image:** Community involvement contributes to the creation of a positive brand image. Real estate investors who are seen as active contributors to local events convey a commitment to the well-being of the community. This positive association can significantly influence the perception of their brand.

- **Connecting on a Personal Level:** Local events provide opportunities for real estate investors to connect with residents on a personal level. Casual interactions at community gatherings allow for meaningful conversations, creating a foundation for genuine relationships that extend beyond transactional engagements.

2. Strategies for Participating in and Contributing to Local Events

Successful community involvement requires thoughtful planning and strategic execution. By choosing the right events, engaging authentically, and contributing meaningfully, real estate investors can maximize the impact of their presence within the community.

- **Identifying Relevant Local Events:** Choosing events that align with the interests and values of the community is crucial. Whether it's a farmers' market, school fair, or environmental cleanup, real estate investors should participate in events that resonate with the local demographic.

- **Authentic Engagement:** Authenticity is key to successful community engagement. Real estate investors should actively participate in events, showing genuine interest in the community's well-being rather than merely viewing events as marketing opportunities.

- **Providing Value to Attendees:** Contributing value to event attendees enhances the impact of community involvement. This could involve sponsoring a local sports team, providing free resources like informational guides, or hosting educational workshops that benefit residents.

- **Creating Lasting Impressions:** Making lasting impressions involves memorable interactions. Whether it's distributing branded giveaways, organizing engaging activities, or offering useful resources, real estate investors can leave a positive and lasting impact on event attendees.

B. Sponsorships and Philanthropy: Integrating Social Responsibility into Marketing

1. The Role of Sponsorships in Community Engagement

Sponsorships form a bridge between real estate investors and the community, providing opportunities for visibility, brand recognition, and meaningful contributions. From supporting local sports teams to sponsoring cultural events, sponsorships showcase a commitment to community enrichment.

- **Enhancing Visibility and Brand Recognition:** Sponsorships enhance visibility within the community. Whether it's placing banners at local events, sponsoring community newsletters, or supporting school programs, real estate investors gain exposure and increased brand recognition through sponsorships.

- **Aligning with Local Values:** Strategic sponsorships align with local values. By sponsoring events or initiatives that resonate with the community's interests, real estate investors demonstrate a genuine understanding of and connection to the values that matter most to residents.

- **Creating Positive Associations:** Positive associations arise from sponsorships that contribute to the community's well-being. Whether it's supporting a charity run, funding a local park renovation, or sponsoring educational programs, these initiatives create positive associations with the real estate professional's brand.

2. Incorporating Philanthropic Initiatives into Marketing Efforts

Philanthropy goes beyond mere sponsorships; it involves actively contributing to the betterment of the community through charitable endeavors. Integrating philanthropic initiatives into marketing efforts underscores a commitment to social responsibility and leaves a lasting impact.

- **Identifying Meaningful Causes:** Choosing philanthropic initiatives that resonate with the community adds depth to marketing efforts. Whether it's supporting local charities, funding educational scholarships, or contributing to environmental conservation, real estate investors should align with causes that matter to residents.

- **Transparent Communication of Contributions:** Transparently communicating philanthropic contributions builds trust. Real estate investors should clearly convey how their contributions positively impact the community, whether through newsletters, social media, or dedicated sections on their website.

- **Collaborative Philanthropy:** Collaborative philanthropy involves engaging the community in charitable endeavors. Real estate investors can organize community-driven initiatives, such as donation drives or volunteer programs, fostering a sense of collective responsibility and shared purpose.

In conclusion, community engagement serves as a cornerstone for real estate investors seeking sustainable success in a competitive market. Actively participating in local events and contributing to community well-being create opportunities to build trust, establish a positive brand image, and connect with residents on a personal level. Sponsorships and philanthropy further amplify the impact, providing avenues for increased visibility, brand recognition, and alignment with local values.

Chapter 6: Leveraging Technology in Real Estate Marketing

Section 1: Real Estate Technology Trends - Shaping the Future of the Industry

In the fast-paced world of real estate, staying abreast of technological advancements is crucial for professionals aiming to remain competitive and provide innovative solutions. This section provides a comprehensive overview of recent and emerging technological trends in the real estate industry, emphasizing the profound impact technology has on the evolution of the sector.

A. Overview of Technological Advancements in the Industry

1. The Dynamic Landscape of Real Estate Technology

The real estate industry is undergoing a profound transformation fueled by technological innovations. From property search and transaction processes to customer engagement and data analytics, technology is reshaping every facet of the real estate ecosystem.

- **PropTech Revolution:** The convergence of real estate and technology, often referred to as PropTech, is driving unprecedented changes. PropTech encompasses a wide array of technologies designed to streamline and enhance various aspects of real estate, from residential and commercial transactions to property management and investment.

- **Cloud-Based Solutions:** Cloud computing has become a cornerstone of real estate technology. The ability to store and access vast amounts of data remotely allows for more efficient collaboration, enhanced security, and the scalability needed to support the industry's evolving demands.

- **Mobile Technologies:** The ubiquity of smartphones has catalyzed the development of mobile applications that empower real estate investors and consumers alike. Mobile technologies facilitate property searches, virtual tours, and communication between stakeholders, fostering a more agile and responsive industry.

2. The Impact of Technology on the Evolution of the Industry

The integration of technology into real estate processes is not merely a trend; it is a transformative force shaping the industry's future. Several key areas highlight the profound impact of technology on the evolution of real estate.

- **Streamlining Transactions:** Technology is simplifying and expediting the traditionally complex process of real estate transactions. Digital platforms facilitate electronic signatures, document sharing, and online closings, reducing paperwork and enhancing the overall efficiency of transactions.

- **Enhanced Data Analytics:** The availability of big data and advanced analytics tools is revolutionizing decision-making in real estate. Professionals can now leverage data to identify market trends, assess property values, and make informed investment decisions, leading to more accurate predictions and risk assessments.

- **Virtual Collaboration and Remote Work:** The rise of virtual collaboration tools and remote work solutions has become particularly relevant in the wake of global shifts in work dynamics. Real estate investors can now collaborate seamlessly with clients, colleagues, and partners regardless of geographical constraints.

B. AI, Virtual Reality, and Blockchain Application

1. Exploring the Role of Artificial Intelligence in Real Estate

Artificial Intelligence (AI) is at the forefront of technological advancements in real estate, offering transformative capabilities that redefine how professionals operate.

- **Automated Property Valuation:** AI algorithms can analyze vast datasets to provide accurate property valuations. Automated valuation models (AVMs) utilize machine learning to assess property values based on factors such as location, market trends, and historical data.

- **Predictive Analytics for Investment:** AI-driven predictive analytics empower real estate investors to forecast market trends, identify investment opportunities, and mitigate risks. Machine learning algorithms analyze historical data to generate insights into potential future outcomes, guiding strategic decision-making.

- **Chatbots and Virtual Assistants:** AI-powered chatbots and virtual assistants are enhancing customer interactions. These intelligent tools can answer inquiries, schedule appointments, and provide personalized property recommendations, offering a seamless and responsive experience for clients.

2. Applications of Virtual Reality and Blockchain Technology

Virtual Reality (VR) and Blockchain are two innovative technologies making substantial inroads into real estate, fundamentally altering how properties are showcased and transactions are conducted.

- **Immersive Property Showcases with Virtual Reality:** Virtual Reality revolutionizes property showcasing by providing immersive virtual tours. Prospective buyers can explore properties remotely, gaining a realistic sense of the space and layout without physically visiting the site.

- **Blockchain in Property Transactions:** Blockchain technology introduces transparency and security to real estate transactions. Smart contracts, powered by blockchain, enable self-executing agreements, reducing the need for intermediaries and enhancing the efficiency and trustworthiness of property transactions.

- **Tokenization of Real Estate Assets:** Blockchain facilitates the tokenization of real estate assets, allowing properties to be divided into tradable digital tokens. This innovation opens up new avenues for fractional ownership, making real estate investment more accessible to a broader range of investors.

In conclusion, the technological landscape of real estate is dynamic and ever-evolving, ushering in an era of unprecedented possibilities. The overview of technological advancements highlights the transformative impact of PropTech, cloud-based solutions, and mobile technologies on the industry. Additionally, the exploration of AI, Virtual Reality, and Blockchain applications underscores the role of these cutting-edge technologies in reshaping key aspects of real estate operations, from property valuation and investment strategies to immersive property showcases and secure transactions.

Section 2: Real Estate Software Tools

A. Utilizing CRM Systems

1. Importance of Customer Relationship Management (CRM) in

Real Estate

Customer Relationship Management (CRM) systems play a pivotal role in real estate marketing, providing a centralized platform to manage interactions, streamline communication, and nurture client relationships.

- **Centralized Contact Management:** CRM systems centralize contact information, communication history, and client preferences. This centralized database enables real estate investors to have a comprehensive view of their clients, facilitating personalized interactions.

- **Lead Tracking and Nurturing:** CRM systems enable effective lead tracking and nurturing. By categorizing leads based on their stage in the buying or selling process, real estate investors can tailor marketing strategies to meet specific needs and timelines.

- **Automated Communication:** Automation features in CRM systems streamline communication workflows. Automated emails, follow-up reminders, and personalized messages ensure consistent and timely engagement with clients, enhancing overall customer satisfaction.

2. Selecting and Implementing CRM Systems for Effective Marketing

Choosing the right CRM system is crucial for successful real estate marketing. The selection process involves considering factors such as features, scalability, integration capabilities, and user-friendliness.

- **Features Tailored for Real Estate:** Real estate-specific CRM systems often come equipped with features tailored to industry needs. These may include property management tools, transaction tracking, and integrations with property listing platforms for seamless data synchronization.

- **Scalability for Growing Businesses:** Scalability is a key consideration when selecting a CRM system. As real estate businesses expand, the CRM should be able to accommodate increased data, users, and functionalities without compromising performance.

- **Integration with Marketing Channels:** Integration capabilities with various marketing channels are essential. A CRM system should seamlessly integrate with email marketing platforms, social media channels, and other tools to ensure cohesive and efficient marketing campaigns.

B. Project Management and Analytics Tools

1. Introduction to Project Management Tools for Marketing Campaigns

Project management tools are instrumental in planning, executing, and monitoring real estate marketing campaigns. These tools enhance collaboration, streamline workflows, and ensure that marketing initiatives are executed successfully.

- **Collaborative Planning and Execution:** Project management tools facilitate collaborative planning and execution. Real estate marketing often involves multiple team members, each handling different aspects of a campaign. These tools provide a centralized platform for planning tasks, setting deadlines, and tracking progress.

- **Task Prioritization and Timeline Management:** Effective marketing campaigns require meticulous task prioritization and timeline management. Project management tools help real estate investors allocate resources, set priorities, and create realistic timelines for each stage of a marketing campaign.

- **Performance Tracking and Analytics:** Analytics tools integrated into project management platforms allow real-time tracking of campaign performance. Key performance indicators (KPIs), such as website traffic, lead generation, and conversion rates, can be monitored to assess the success of marketing efforts.

2. Utilizing Analytics Tools to Measure and Optimize Marketing Performance

Analytics tools provide valuable insights that empower real estate investors to measure, analyze, and optimize their marketing performance, ensuring continuous improvement and increased effectiveness.

- **Key Metrics for Real Estate Marketing:** Identifying and monitoring key metrics is crucial for assessing the impact of marketing efforts. Metrics such as website traffic, conversion rates, lead sources, and engagement levels help real estate investors make data-driven decisions.

- **A/B Testing for Optimization:** A/B testing involves comparing two versions of a marketing element (such as an email subject line or a website landing page) to determine which performs better. This iterative testing process allows real estate investors to refine their strategies based on data-driven insights.

- **Feedback Loops for Continuous Improvement:** Implementing feedback loops within analytics tools creates a continuous improvement cycle. Real estate investors can gather feedback from various sources, including client interactions, website analytics, and campaign performance, to refine and optimize their marketing strategies over time.

In conclusion, the integration of technology in real estate marketing has ushered in a new era of efficiency, connectivity, and innovation. From the application of AI and VR to the utilization of CRM systems and analytics tools, real estate investors can leverage these technological advancements to enhance their marketing strategies and adapt to the evolving needs of the industry. As the digital landscape continues to evolve, staying abreast of technological trends and incorporating these tools strategically will be essential for sustained success in real estate marketing.

Section 3: Automation in Marketing

Automation in real estate marketing has emerged as a transformative force, revolutionizing the way tasks are executed, campaigns are managed, and customer interactions are handled. This section explores the significance of streamlining repetitive marketing tasks and delves into the implementation of marketing automation platforms. By understanding the benefits and strategies associated with automation, real estate investors can enhance efficiency, reduce manual workload, and create more targeted and personalized marketing experiences for their audience.

A. Streamlining Repetitive Marketing Task

1. Identifying Tasks Suitable for Automation in Real Estate Marketing

Repetitive marketing tasks are inherent in the real estate industry, from email communications and social media postings to lead nurturing and data management. Identifying tasks that are suitable for automation is a crucial first step in streamlining operations and freeing up valuable time for strategic planning and relationship-building.

- **Email Campaigns and Drip Sequences:** Automating email campaigns and drip sequences allows real estate investors to maintain consistent communication with leads and clients. This includes sending out newsletters, property updates, and personalized messages at predetermined intervals.

- **Social Media Posting and Scheduling:** Social media is a powerful tool for real estate marketing, but consistent posting can be time-consuming. Automation tools enable the scheduling of posts in advance, ensuring a steady and engaging online presence without the need for manual intervention.

- **Lead Scoring and Qualification:** Automation can be applied to lead scoring and qualification processes. By setting predefined criteria, automation tools can analyze lead behavior, assign scores, and determine the level of engagement, allowing real estate investors to prioritize their efforts on leads with higher conversion potential.

- **Data Entry and Management:** Handling large volumes of data is a common challenge in real estate. Automation can streamline data entry processes, ensuring accurate and up-to-date information in CRM systems, and reducing the risk of errors associated with manual data input.

2. Efficiency Gains Through Task Automation

The primary advantage of streamlining repetitive marketing tasks through automation lies in the efficiency gains it brings to real estate investors. By automating time-consuming and routine activities, professionals can redirect their focus towards high-value tasks that require creativity, strategic thinking, and personalized engagement.

- **Time Savings for Strategic Planning:** Automating repetitive tasks liberates time for real estate investors to engage in strategic planning and goal setting and actual deal activity. This shift from manual execution to strategic thinking allows for a more proactive and forward-looking approach to marketing.

- **Consistency in Marketing Efforts:** Automation ensures consistency in marketing efforts. From scheduled social media posts to regular email communications, the automated execution of tasks reduces the likelihood of lapses, ensuring that marketing campaigns run smoothly and adhere to predefined schedules.

- **Scalability of Marketing Operations:** As your real estate businesses grow, the demand for scalable marketing operations increases. Automation facilitates scalability by handling repetitive tasks efficiently, allowing businesses to expand their reach, manage larger client databases, and execute more complex marketing campaigns without proportionally increasing the workload.

B. Implementing Marketing Automation Platforms

1. Overview of Marketing Automation Platforms

Marketing automation platforms are comprehensive tools designed to automate, streamline, and optimize various aspects of marketing campaigns. These platforms offer a range of features, including email automation, lead management, analytics, and integration capabilities with other tools and systems.

Key Features of Marketing Automation Platforms

Marketing automation platforms typically encompass a suite of features tailored to meet the diverse needs of real estate investors:

- *Email Marketing Automation:* Automated email campaigns, personalized drip sequences, and triggered responses based on lead behavior are common features in marketing automation platforms. These capabilities enhance the efficiency of email marketing efforts.

- *Lead Scoring and Nurturing:* Marketing automation platforms often include lead scoring mechanisms that assess lead engagement and assign scores based on predefined criteria. Nurturing features facilitate the delivery of targeted content to leads at different stages of the buying or selling journey.

- *Workflow Automation:* Workflow automation streamlines processes by creating predefined workflows for various marketing tasks. This includes automating data entry, assigning tasks to team members, and triggering specific actions based on user interactions.

- *Analytics and Reporting:* Robust analytics and reporting tools provide real-time insights into the performance of marketing campaigns. Metrics such as open rates, click-through rates, and conversion rates enable data-driven decision-making.

2. Strategies for Successful Implementation and Utilization

While the adoption of marketing automation platforms offers significant benefits, successful implementation requires careful planning, strategic utilization, and ongoing optimization. Real estate investors can maximize the impact of these platforms by following key strategies.

- **Define Clear Objectives and Workflows:** Before implementing a marketing automation platform, it is essential to define clear objectives and workflows. This involves mapping out the customer journey, identifying touchpoints, and outlining the desired outcomes at each stage.

- **Segmentation for Personalized Communication:** Effective segmentation is a cornerstone of successful marketing automation. By segmenting leads and clients based on criteria such as behavior, demographics, or preferences, real estate investors can deliver personalized and relevant content that resonates with the audience.

- **Integration with Existing Systems:** Integration with existing systems, such as CRM platforms and website analytics tools, ensures seamless data flow and consistency across different tools. This integration enhances the overall efficiency and effectiveness of marketing operations.

- **Continuous Monitoring and Optimization:** Marketing automation is not a set-it-and-forget-it solution. Continuous monitoring of campaign performance, analyzing data, and optimizing workflows are crucial for adapting to changing market dynamics and ensuring ongoing success.

- **Training and Skill Development:** Training team members on the effective use of marketing automation platforms is essential for maximizing their potential. Investing in skill development ensures that the team can leverage the full range of features and functionalities offered by the platform.

In conclusion, automation has become a cornerstone of modern real estate marketing, providing professionals with the tools to streamline operations, enhance efficiency, and deliver more personalized and targeted experiences to their audience. By identifying tasks suitable for automation, real estate investors can unlock time for strategic planning and relationship-building. Additionally, the implementation of marketing automation platforms offers a comprehensive solution to manage campaigns, nurture leads, and analyze performance, contributing to sustained success in an increasingly competitive industry.

Section 4: Virtual Tours and Digital Showings

Advancements in technology have transformed the way properties are presented and showcased in the real estate industry. This section explores the impact of virtual tours and digital showings on property marketing. From enhancing property presentations through immersive experiences to exploring the applications of virtual reality (VR) and 3D tours, real estate investors can leverage these technologies to provide prospective buyers with a more interactive and engaging viewing experience.

A. Enhancing Property Presentations Through Technology

1. The Role of Virtual Tours in Property Marketing

Virtual tours have become a cornerstone of modern property marketing, offering a dynamic and immersive way for potential buyers to explore homes and commercial spaces. The traditional approach of static images is complemented, if not replaced, by interactive virtual tours that provide a more realistic representation of the property.

- **Immersive Experiences for Prospective Buyers:** Virtual tours enable prospective buyers to virtually navigate through a property, exploring each room and space as if they were physically present. This immersive experience creates a deeper connection with the property, allowing buyers to envision themselves in the space.

- **Increased Engagement and Time on Listing:** The interactive nature of virtual tours leads to increased engagement and longer viewing times on property listings. Potential buyers can take their time exploring the details of a property, from the layout of rooms to specific features, fostering a more informed decision-making process.

- **Appealing to Remote and International Buyers:** Virtual tours cater to the needs of remote and international buyers who may not have the opportunity to visit properties in person. By providing a comprehensive virtual experience, real estate investors can attract a broader audience and facilitate long-distance property transactions.

2. Utilizing Technology for Immersive Property Presentations

Technology plays a crucial role in creating immersive property presentations that go beyond traditional photography. Various tools and techniques contribute to the development of compelling virtual tours.

- **High-Quality Photography and Videography:** High-quality visuals are the foundation of any successful virtual tour. Professional photography and videography capture the essence of a property, showcasing its features and unique selling points in the best possible light.

- **Interactive Floor Plans and Navigation:** Interactive floor plans enhance the user experience by providing a clear layout of the property. Navigation features allow users to move seamlessly from room to room, providing a sense of the property's flow and spatial organization.

- **360-Degree Views and Panoramas:** 360-degree views and panoramas offer a comprehensive look at the surroundings from different vantage points. This feature adds depth to the virtual tour, allowing viewers to explore the property from various angles.

B. Virtual Reality and 3D Tours

1. Exploring Virtual Reality Applications in Real Estate:

Virtual reality (VR) takes the concept of virtual tours to the next level by creating a fully immersive experience. By donning VR headsets, potential buyers can virtually step into a property and explore it in a more realistic and interactive manner.

- **Creating a Sense of Presence:** VR applications in real estate create a sense of presence, allowing users to feel as if they are physically present in the property. This heightened level of immersion contributes to a more emotional and memorable experience.

- **Remote Property Viewing with VR Headsets:** VR headsets enable remote property viewing, giving buyers the ability to tour a property from the comfort of their homes. This is particularly valuable for international buyers or those unable to attend in-person showings.

- **Virtual Staging and Customization:** Virtual reality allows for virtual staging and customization, where users can visualize different design options and configurations. This feature enhances the personalization of the property viewing experience.

2. Creating Engaging 3D Tours for Property Showcases

3D tours provide a detailed and realistic representation of a property, offering viewers a comprehensive understanding of its layout and features.

- **360-Degree Panoramic Views:** Similar to virtual tours, 3D tours often incorporate 360-degree panoramic views, enabling viewers to look around and explore the property from different perspectives.

- **Annotation and Information Integration:** Annotations and information integration within 3D tours enhance the educational aspect of the property showcase. Users can access details about specific features or highlights as they navigate through the tour.

- **Compatibility with Multiple Devices:** 3D tours are designed to be compatible with various devices, including computers, tablets, and smartphones. This flexibility ensures accessibility for a wide range of users.

In conclusion, virtual tours and digital showings have become integral components of modern real estate marketing, providing a dynamic and interactive means of showcasing properties. From immersive virtual tours that allow users to explore every corner of a property to the advanced experiences offered by virtual reality and 3D tours, these technologies enhance the buyer's journey and contribute to more informed and confident purchasing decisions. Real estate investors who embrace and strategically implement these technologies stand to gain a competitive edge in a market where visual engagement and immersive experiences are increasingly valued by prospective buyers.

Section 5: Cybersecurity in Real Estate Marketing

As the real estate industry continues to embrace digital transformation, the importance of cybersecurity in real estate marketing becomes increasingly paramount. This section explores the critical aspects of protecting sensitive data and implementing best practices for securing online transactions. As real estate investors leverage technology for marketing, it is crucial to prioritize cybersecurity to safeguard client information, maintain trust, and uphold the integrity of online transactions.

A. Protecting Sensitive Data

1. Importance of Data Security in Real Estate Marketing

In an era where data is a valuable asset, real estate investors handle vast amounts of sensitive information, including client details, property records, and financial transactions. The importance of data security in real estate marketing cannot be overstated, as breaches can lead to severe consequences, including financial losses, reputational damage, and legal implications.

- **Client Confidentiality and Trust:** Upholding client confidentiality is a cornerstone of trust in the real estate industry. Clients entrust real estate investors with sensitive information, and ensuring the security of this data is not only a legal obligation but also a fundamental element of maintaining a trustworthy reputation.

- **Legal and Compliance Requirements:** Real estate transactions involve compliance with various regulations and legal requirements. Protecting sensitive data is not just good practice; it is often mandated by laws such as the General Data Protection Regulation (GDPR) and industry-specific regulations governing the protection of client information.

- **Preventing Identity Theft and Fraud:** Real estate transactions involve significant financial transactions, making them potential targets for identity theft and fraud. Cybersecurity measures are essential to prevent unauthorized access, financial manipulation, and fraudulent activities that can compromise the integrity of real estate transactions.

2. Safeguarding Client Information and Transaction Data

Implementing robust cybersecurity measures involves a multifaceted approach to safeguard client information and transaction data throughout the real estate marketing process.

- **Secure Storage and Access Control:** Utilizing secure storage systems and implementing access controls ensures that client information is stored safely and can only be accessed by authorized personnel. This involves encryption, password protection, and role-based access to sensitive data.

- **Regular Security Audits and Assessments:** Conducting regular security audits and assessments helps identify vulnerabilities in systems and processes. These proactive measures enable real estate investors to address potential risks before they can be exploited by cyber threats.

- **Employee Training and Awareness:** Human error is a common factor in cybersecurity breaches. Training and raising awareness among employees about cybersecurity best practices, recognizing phishing attempts, and adhering to security protocols contribute significantly to overall data protection.

B. Best Practices for Securing Online Transactions

1. Strategies for Secure Online Transactions in Real Estate

Online transactions in real estate, including digital signings and financial transactions, require specific strategies to ensure their security.

- **Encryption for Data Transmission:** Implementing encryption protocols for data transmission protects information as it travels across networks. Secure communication channels, such as Secure Sockets

Layer (SSL) or Transport Layer Security (TLS), encrypt data to prevent interception by unauthorized parties.

- **Multi-Factor Authentication (MFA):** Multi-factor authentication adds an extra layer of security by requiring users to verify their identity through multiple steps, such as entering a password and confirming their identity through a mobile app or email. This reduces the risk of unauthorized access.

- **Secure Payment Gateways:** For real estate transactions involving financial payments, using secure payment gateways is essential. These gateways employ encryption and other security measures to protect financial transactions, providing a secure environment for online payments.

2. Implementing Encryption and Secure Communication Protocols

The implementation of encryption and secure communication protocols is critical in securing online transactions and communication channels.

- **End-to-End Encryption:** End-to-end encryption ensures that data is encrypted from the point of origin to its final destination, preventing unauthorized access at any point along the communication path. This level of encryption is particularly crucial for sensitive transactions and communications in real estate.

- **Secure Document Sharing Platforms:** Real estate investors often share sensitive documents during transactions. Utilizing secure document-sharing platforms with encryption features ensures that confidential information remains protected throughout the document exchange process.

- **Regular Updates and Patch Management:** Keeping software, systems, and applications up-to-date with the latest security patches is vital for maintaining a secure environment. Regular updates address vulnerabilities and strengthen defenses against emerging cyber threats.

In conclusion, cybersecurity is a foundational element of real estate marketing in the digital age. As technology plays an increasingly prominent role in the industry, real estate investors must prioritize the protection of sensitive data and the implementation of best practices for securing online transactions. By fostering a culture of cybersecurity awareness, employing robust protective measures, and staying abreast of evolving threats, real estate investors can navigate the digital landscape with confidence, safeguarding both client trust and the integrity of their transactions.

Chapter 7: Crafting Compelling Property Listings

Section 1: Importance of Effective Property Listings

Effective property listings are the cornerstone of successful real estate marketing. In this section, we explore the paramount importance of property listings, their central role in attracting potential buyers or tenants, and the essential elements that make a property listing compelling.

A. Understanding the Role of Listings in Marketing

In the dynamic and competitive real estate market, property listings play a pivotal role in marketing strategies. These listings serve as the initial point of contact between a property and potential buyers or tenants. Key aspects to consider:

- **First Impressions:** Listings often form the first impression buyers or tenants have of a property. A well-crafted listing can generate interest and curiosity.

- **Visibility:** Listings enhance a property's visibility across various platforms, including online listings, social media, and real estate portals.

- **Information Conduit:** Listings are not merely advertisements; they are information conduits that convey crucial details about a property, influencing the decision-making process.

B. Elements of a Compelling Property Listing:

Creating a compelling property listing involves a nuanced approach that goes beyond mere descriptions. It requires careful consideration of various elements:

1. Identifying Key Components

- *High-Quality Visuals:* The inclusion of professional photographs and, where applicable, virtual tours, elevates the visual appeal of the online listing.

- *Accurate Property Descriptions:* Detailed yet concise property descriptions that highlight key features without overwhelming potential buyers or tenants.

- *Clear Call-to-Action:* Including a clear call-to-action guides the reader on the next steps, whether it's scheduling a viewing, contacting an agent, or exploring more details.

- *Strategic Use of Keywords:* Incorporating relevant keywords enhances the listing's visibility in online searches.

2, Crafting Attention-Grabbing Headlines

- *Captivating Headlines:* Headlines are the first thing potential buyers or tenants notice. Crafting headlines that are both attention-grabbing and informative is crucial.

- *Incorporating Key Selling Points:* Headlines should succinctly communicate the property's unique selling points to entice the reader to delve deeper.

3. Concise Property Descriptions

- *Balancing Details and Brevity:* Striking the right balance between providing essential details and maintaining brevity is an art. Buyers or tenants should be able to grasp the property's essence quickly.

- *Storytelling Elements:* Incorporating storytelling elements in property descriptions can create an emotional connection and make the listing more memorable.

Conclusion:

In conclusion, the importance of effective property listings cannot be overstated in the realm of real estate marketing. They serve as the bridge between properties and potential buyers or tenants, influencing decisions and shaping perceptions. Crafting compelling listings involves a thoughtful combination of visual appeal, strategic messaging, and an understanding of the target audience.

Section 2: Professional Photography and Videography

In the highly visual realm of real estate marketing, where first impressions are crucial, the impact of professional photography and videography cannot be overstated. This section explores the importance of creating visually appealing property content and the significant role that hiring professionals plays in ensuring high-quality visuals that effectively showcase properties.

A. Creating Visually Appealing Property Content

1. The Significance of High-Quality Visuals in Property Marketing

Visual content is a cornerstone of property marketing, acting as the first point of contact for potential buyers or tenants. High-quality visuals not only capture attention but also convey the essence and unique features of a property. In a competitive market, where online browsing often precedes physical visits, compelling visuals serve as powerful tools to pique interest and leave a lasting impression.

- **The Power of Visual Appeal:** Visual appeal goes beyond mere aesthetics; it has a psychological impact on viewers. Engaging visuals create an emotional connection with the property, fostering a sense of desire and aspiration in potential buyers or tenants.

- **Enhancing Perception of Property Value:** Professionally captured visuals contribute to the perceived value of a property. Quality photography and videography can make spaces appear more spacious, well-lit, and inviting, positively influencing the perceived value of the property.

- **Setting the Tone for Property Showcasing:** Visual content sets the tone for how a property is perceived. Whether highlighting the cozy ambiance of a home, the modern design of a condominium, or the spacious layout of a commercial space, visuals convey the narrative that shapes potential buyers' or tenants' expectations.

- **Online Browsing and Virtual Impressions:** In the digital age, property searches often begin online. Engaging and high-quality visuals serve as a virtual introduction, enticing viewers to explore further and, ideally, schedule a physical visit.

2. Tips for Capturing the Essence of a Property Through

Photography

While professional photographers bring expertise to the table, property owners and real estate investors can play a role in ensuring the best possible visuals. Understanding key considerations for capturing the essence of a property through photography contributes to a collaborative and effective visual marketing strategy.

- **Showcasing Key Features:** Identify and prioritize the key features of a property. Whether it's a gourmet kitchen, a spacious backyard, or panoramic views, these features should be prominently showcased in the visuals.

- **Lighting Matters:** Adequate lighting is paramount in photography. Ensure that spaces are well-lit to capture their full potential. Natural light is often preferred for creating a bright and inviting atmosphere.

- **Declutter and Stage:** Before the photoshoot, decluttering and staging the property can significantly enhance its visual appeal. Clearing spaces of unnecessary items allows potential buyers or tenants to envision the property as a blank canvas for their preferences.

- **Angles and Perspectives:** Experiment with different angles and perspectives to showcase the property from its best vantage points. This includes capturing both wide-angle shots to convey overall layouts and detailed close-ups to highlight specific features.

B. Hiring Professionals for High-Quality Visuals

1. The Role of Professional Photographers and Videographers

While property owners or real estate investors may have smartphones with impressive cameras, the expertise of professional photographers and videographers brings a level of skill, artistry, and technical know-how that elevates the visual representation of a property.

- **Technical Expertise:** Professional photographers and videographers possess the technical skills to capture images in various lighting conditions, handle equipment effectively, and edit visuals to perfection. Their expertise ensures a polished and professional presentation.

- **Understanding Real Estate Dynamics:** Professionals specializing in real estate photography understand the unique dynamics of property marketing. They know how to highlight the features that resonate with potential buyers or tenants and showcase properties in a way that aligns with market trends.

- **Equipment and Editing Tools:** Professional photographers invest in high-quality equipment, including cameras, lenses, and lighting tools, to capture the best possible visuals. Additionally, they often use advanced editing tools to enhance images and create a visually stunning final product.

- **Time Efficiency:** Time is often of the essence in real estate transactions. Professional photographers work efficiently, ensuring that the property is captured at its best without unnecessary delays. Quick turnaround times are crucial in maintaining momentum in the marketing process.

2. Choosing the Right Professionals to Showcase Properties Effectively

Selecting the right professionals for photography and videography is a critical decision that impacts the overall success of a property marketing campaign. Considerations such as experience, portfolio, and collaboration dynamics play a significant role in making an informed choice.

- **Reviewing Portfolios:** Evaluate the portfolios of prospective photographers and videographers. Look for consistency in quality, an understanding of diverse property types, and an ability to capture a range of architectural styles.

- **Experience in Real Estate Photography:** Prioritize professionals with experience specifically in real estate photography. Familiarity with the unique requirements of property marketing ensures that the visuals align with industry standards and effectively communicate the property's appeal.

- **Collaboration and Communication Skills:** Effective collaboration between property owners, real estate investors, and visual content creators is essential. Choose professionals who demonstrate strong communication skills, understand client preferences, and can adapt to specific marketing objectives.

- **Client Testimonials and Referrals:** Seek client testimonials and referrals from other real estate investors or property owners who have worked with the photographers or videographers under consideration. Positive feedback and successful collaborations are indicators of reliability and professionalism.

In conclusion, the visual presentation of properties through professional photography and videography is a cornerstone of effective real estate marketing. Understanding the significance of high-quality visuals and the role of professionals in creating them empowers property owners and real estate investors to make informed decisions that enhance the overall impact of their marketing campaigns.

Section 3: Writing Engaging Property Descriptions

Effective property listings are the cornerstone of successful real estate marketing. In this section, we explore the art and science of crafting persuasive and descriptive property narratives. From techniques for writing compelling descriptions to the use of storytelling elements, this segment provides valuable insights for real estate investors seeking to enhance the impact of their property listings.

A. Crafting Persuasive and Descriptive Property Narratives

1. Techniques for Writing Compelling Property Descriptions

Crafting a compelling property description goes beyond listing features; it involves creating a narrative that captivates potential buyers or tenants. Here are key techniques to elevate property descriptions:

- **Highlight Unique Selling Points:** Identify and emphasize the unique selling points of the property. Whether it's a stunning view, modern amenities, or a spacious layout, these features should take center stage in the description.

- **Use Descriptive Language:** Paint a vivid picture with descriptive language. Instead of generic terms, use adjectives that evoke emotion and provide a sensory experience. For example, replace "spacious living room" with "expansive, sunlit living space perfect for entertaining."

- **Address Lifestyle Benefits:** Connect the property features to the lifestyle benefits they offer. If the kitchen is equipped with state-of-the-art appliances, highlight how it makes daily cooking a pleasure or enhances the overall culinary experience.

- **Create a Sense of Urgency:** Introduce a sense of urgency without pressure. Phrases like "rare opportunity," "limited availability," or "exclusive offer" can motivate potential buyers or tenants to take prompt action.

- **Provide Context:** Offer context about the neighborhood, nearby amenities, and the overall community. This helps potential buyers envision the complete lifestyle associated with the property.

2. Balancing Details and Brevity to Maintain Reader Engagement

Striking the right balance between providing detailed information and maintaining brevity is crucial for reader engagement. While it's essential to convey pertinent details, overly long descriptions can lead to disinterest. Here's how to achieve the right balance:

- **Prioritize Key Features:** Identify the key features that are likely to resonate most with the target audience. Focus on these features while keeping the overall description concise.

- **Use Bullet Points for Quick Scanning:** Break down key information into bullet points. This makes it easier for potential buyers or tenants to quickly scan the listing while still grasping the essential details.

- **Create Sections for Different Aspects:** Divide the property description into sections addressing different aspects, such as interior features, outdoor amenities, and neighborhood highlights. This helps organize information and guides readers through the content.

- **Encourage Further Exploration:** Instead of overwhelming readers with exhaustive details, entice them to learn more. Include a call-to-action inviting interested parties to contact for additional information, schedule a viewing, or explore more photos and details on a dedicated website or listing platform.

B. Utilizing Storytelling Techniques

1. Incorporating Storytelling Elements to Evoke Emotion

Storytelling has a powerful impact on engaging emotions and creating a connection. In real estate, weaving a narrative around a property can elevate its perceived value and resonate with potential buyers or tenants. Consider the following storytelling elements:

- **Create a Narrative Arc:** Structure the property description like a story with a beginning, middle, and end. Start by introducing the property, delve into its unique features in the middle, and conclude with a compelling reason why it's the ideal choice.

- **Focus on Lifestyle Scenarios:** Craft scenarios that showcase the property in real-life situations. For example, describe a family gathering in the spacious backyard, or paint a picture of a cozy evening by the fireplace.

- **Use Imagery-Driven Language:** Engage the reader's imagination by incorporating imagery-driven language. Instead of simply stating facts, use descriptive words that conjure mental images, allowing potential buyers or tenants to visualize themselves in the space.

- **Tell Success Stories:** Share success stories or positive experiences associated with the property. This could include previous happy occupants, successful events hosted at the property, or any unique achievements attributed to the space.

2. Creating a Narrative that Resonates with Potential Buyers or Tenants

The ultimate goal of incorporating storytelling techniques is to create a narrative that resonates with the target audience. Align the narrative with the lifestyle aspirations and preferences of potential buyers or tenants:

- **Understand Your Target Audience:** Tailor the narrative to match the preferences and aspirations of the target demographic. Whether it's a family seeking a serene retreat or young professionals looking for a vibrant urban lifestyle, the narrative should speak to their desires.

- **Highlight Emotional Benefits:** Move beyond the physical features and highlight the emotional benefits of living in the property. This could include feelings of comfort, security, community, or accomplishment associated with the space.

- **Invoke a Sense of Belonging:** Craft the narrative to make potential buyers or tenants feel a sense of belonging. Use language that communicates how the property is not just a structure but a place where they can create lasting memories and build a fulfilling life.

- **Showcase Future Possibilities:** Inspire potential buyers or tenants by showcasing the future possibilities the property offers. Whether it's room for expansion, a flexible layout for various uses, or proximity to upcoming developments, illustrate how the property aligns with their future goals.

In conclusion, mastering the art of crafting compelling property listings involves a combination of effective writing techniques and strategic storytelling. By incorporating persuasive language, highlighting unique selling points, and creating narratives that resonate emotionally, real estate investors can elevate their listings to stand out in a competitive market. Balancing details with brevity ensures that the information is easily digestible, capturing the attention of potential buyers or tenants. With a well-crafted property description, a listing can become a powerful tool for attracting the right audience and driving successful real estate transactions.

Section 4: Highlighting Unique Selling Points

Highlighting unique selling points is a critical aspect of creating compelling property listings that capture the attention of potential buyers or tenants. In this section, we delve into effective strategies for identifying and showcasing the strengths of a property, as well as differentiating your listings from competitors in a competitive real estate market.

A. Identifying and Showcasing Property Strengths

1. Strategies for Identifying Unique Selling Points in a Property

Before crafting a property listing, it's essential to identify and understand the unique selling points (USPs) that make a property stand out. Here are strategies to pinpoint and showcase these strengths:

- **Conduct a Thorough Property Inspection:** Begin by conducting a comprehensive inspection of the property. Look beyond standard features and assess any unique architectural elements, design aspects, or built-in amenities that contribute to its appeal.

- **Consider Location-specific Advantages:** Evaluate the property's location-specific advantages. Proximity to amenities, scenic views, accessibility to transportation hubs, and the overall neighborhood ambiance are crucial factors that can serve as significant selling points.

- **Gather Feedback from Current or Previous Occupants:** If possible, gather feedback from current or previous occupants. Understand their perspectives on what makes the property special. This insight can uncover hidden strengths that may not be immediately apparent.

- **Highlight Energy Efficiency and Sustainability:** In today's market, energy efficiency and sustainability are often valued selling points. If the property incorporates eco-friendly features, such as solar panels, energy-efficient appliances, or sustainable landscaping, emphasize these aspects.

- **Showcase Renovations and Upgrades:** If the property has undergone recent renovations or includes upgraded features, showcase these improvements. Modern amenities, updated kitchens or bathrooms, and smart home technologies are appealing to many buyers or tenants.

2. Showcasing Features that Set the Property Apart from Others in the Market

Once identified, the unique selling points must be effectively showcased in the property listing. Here's how to highlight features that set the property apart from others in the market:

- **Create a Compelling Headline:** Craft a headline that immediately captures attention and conveys a standout feature. Whether it's a breathtaking view, architectural uniqueness, or a luxurious amenity, the headline should entice readers to explore further.

- **Utilize Visually Engaging Media:** Leverage high-quality visuals, including professional photographs and videos, to showcase unique selling points. Visual media allows potential buyers or tenants to get a firsthand look at the distinctive features that make the property special.

- **Incorporate Descriptive Language:** Use descriptive language in the property description to convey the essence of unique features. Instead of merely listing attributes, tell a story that brings these features to life, allowing potential buyers or tenants to envision themselves in the space.

- **Provide Context for Lifestyle Enhancement:** Connect unique selling points to lifestyle enhancements. For example, if the property features a spacious outdoor deck, highlight how it provides an ideal space for entertaining guests or enjoying tranquil evenings.

- **Offer Comparative Advantages:** Clearly articulate how the property's unique selling points compare favorably to others in the market. Whether it's superior craftsmanship, innovative design, or exclusive amenities, emphasize what sets the property apart.

B. Differentiating Your Listings from Competitors

1. Analyzing Competitor Listings for Differentiation

To effectively differentiate your listings, a thorough analysis of competitor listings is essential. Here's how to conduct a strategic assessment:

- **Identify Common Trends:** Start by identifying common trends or features in competitor listings within the same market or category. This analysis helps identify industry norms and provides a baseline for differentiation.

- **Assess Unique Offerings:** Evaluate unique offerings featured in competitor listings. This could include special promotions, added-value services, or distinctive property features. Identify areas where competitors may be excelling or lacking.

- **Understand Target Audience Preferences:** Gain insights into the preferences of the target audience shared by competitors. Recognizing common themes or amenities that resonate with potential buyers or tenants allows for strategic differentiation.

- **Evaluate Presentation Styles:** Analyze the presentation styles adopted by competitors. This includes the use of visuals, tone of language, and overall branding. Identify elements that contribute to a positive reception and those that may be improved upon.

2. Developing a Unique Selling Proposition for Your Properties

Armed with insights from competitor analysis, focus on developing a unique selling proposition (USP) for your properties. Here's how to create a compelling USP:

- **Identify Core Strengths:** Determine the core strengths of your properties that align with market demand. These strengths could be related to property features, pricing structures, or unique services offered.

- **Emphasize Value Proposition:** Clearly articulate the value proposition your properties offer. Whether it's affordability, luxury, convenience, or a combination of factors, emphasize what sets your listings apart and adds value for potential buyers or tenants.

- **Highlight Exceptional Services:** If your real estate services go beyond the standard, highlight these exceptional offerings. This could include personalized property tours, dedicated customer support, or innovative marketing strategies.

- **Craft a Distinctive Brand Image:** Develop a distinctive brand image that resonates with your target audience. Consistent branding across listings creates a recognizable identity and reinforces the unique qualities associated with your properties.

- **Communicate a Compelling Story:** Weave a compelling narrative around your properties. Tell a story that goes beyond the physical attributes and communicates the lifestyle, aspirations, and experiences associated with choosing your listings.

In conclusion, the success of a property listing hinges on effectively showcasing its *unique selling points* and differentiating it from competitors. By employing strategic techniques to identify, highlight, and communicate the strengths of a property, real estate investors can create listings that stand out in a crowded market. Understanding the preferences of the target audience and strategically positioning your properties through a well-defined unique selling proposition ensures that your listings not only capture attention but also resonate with potential buyers or tenants, ultimately leading to successful real estate transactions.

Section 5: A/B Testing for Optimization

Effective real estate marketing involves continuous improvement and optimization of listing elements to enhance performance. In this section, we explore the concept of A/B testing for property listings, providing insights into testing and refining different elements to maximize listing performance. Additionally, we delve into the importance of data analysis in leveraging metrics for iterative refinement.

A. Testing and Refining Listing Elements

1. Introduction to A/B Testing for Property Listings

A/B testing, also known as split testing, is a method used to compare two versions of a webpage or, in the context of real estate, a property listing. By presenting two variations (A and B) to different segments of your audience and analyzing which performs better, real estate investors can make informed decisions on optimizing listing elements. Key elements to consider for A/B testing in property listings include:

- **Headlines and Copy:** Test different headlines and copy variations to determine which language resonates best with your target audience. This could involve experimenting with tone, word choice, or the overall messaging approach.

- **Visuals and Media:** Assess the impact of visuals, including photographs and videos, by testing different media formats and compositions. This could involve evaluating the effectiveness of professional photography versus virtual tours or assessing the impact of including lifestyle images.

- **Call-to-Action (CTA):** Evaluate the performance of different calls-to-action. Experiment with variations in language, placement, or design to determine which encourages desired actions, such as property inquiries or scheduling viewings.

- **Property Descriptions:** Test variations in property descriptions, including length, style, and formatting. Determine whether concise or detailed descriptions, storytelling approaches, or feature-focused content lead to higher engagement.

- **Pricing and Offers:** Experiment with different pricing strategies or promotional offers. Assess whether presenting pricing information upfront, using specific pricing structures, or incorporating limited-time offers influences audience response.

2. Experimenting with Different Elements to Optimize Listing Performance

A/B testing provides an opportunity to experiment with various listing elements to identify the most effective combination. Here's how to conduct experiments to optimize listing performance:

- **Define Clear Hypotheses:** Before initiating A/B tests, establish clear hypotheses about the expected impact of changes. Whether testing a new headline or adjusting visual elements, articulate the anticipated outcomes to guide the testing process.

- **Segment Your Audience:** Divide your target audience into segments for A/B testing. Ensure that the segments are representative and comparable to obtain meaningful insights. This could involve testing variations with specific demographic characteristics or behavioral traits.

- **Randomized Testing:** Implement randomized testing to ensure unbiased results. Randomly assign individuals within the target audience segments to either the control group (Version A) or the experimental group (Version B).

- **Collect Quantitative and Qualitative Data:** Gather both quantitative and qualitative data during the testing period. Quantitative metrics may include click-through rates, conversion rates, and engagement metrics. Additionally, gather qualitative feedback through surveys or user interviews to gain insights into user preferences.

- **Monitor and Analyze Results:** Continuously monitor the results of A/B tests. Analyze the performance metrics to determine which version of the listing elements is more effective in achieving the desired outcomes. Consider factors such as user engagement, lead generation, and conversion rates.

B. Maximizing Listing Performance Through Data Analysis

1. Utilizing Data Analytics to Measure the Effectiveness of Listing Elements

Data analytics plays a crucial role in measuring the effectiveness of listing elements. Here's how real estate investors can leverage data analytics to gain insights into listing performance:

- **Implement Tracking Mechanisms:** Use tracking mechanisms, such as analytics tools and conversion tracking, to monitor user interactions with property listings. This includes tracking clicks on CTA buttons, time spent on the listing page, and the number of inquiries generated.

- **Evaluate Conversion Funnel:** Analyze the conversion funnel to understand how users progress from viewing a listing to taking desired actions. Identify potential bottlenecks or points of drop-off in the conversion process.

- **Segmentation Analysis:** Conduct segmentation analysis to identify patterns among different audience segments. This could involve analyzing the performance of listing elements among distinct demographics, geographic locations, or device types.

- **Heatmap Analysis:** Use heatmap analysis to visualize user engagement on listing pages. Heatmaps provide insights into areas of the page that attract the most attention, helping optimize the placement of critical elements such as CTA buttons or property images.

2. Iterative Refinement Based on Performance Metrics

Based on the insights gathered from A/B testing and data analytics, real estate investors can engage in iterative refinement to continuously enhance listing performance. Here's how to iteratively refine listings:

- **Implement Successful Variations:** Identify the variations that outperform others in terms of user engagement, lead generation, or conversion rates. Implement the successful variations as standard elements in future listings.

- **Address Identified Weaknesses:** Address any weaknesses or points of improvement identified during the testing process. Whether it's refining messaging, adjusting visual elements, or optimizing user experience, prioritize enhancements that align with user preferences.

- **Stay Informed About Industry Trends:** Stay informed about industry trends and evolving user preferences. As market dynamics change, regularly assess and update listing elements to align with current expectations and demands.

- **Encourage User Feedback:** Actively seek user feedback to understand their experiences with property listings. Incorporate constructive feedback into the refinement process, ensuring that listings align with the evolving needs and preferences of the target audience.

- **Continuously Experiment:** Maintain a mindset of continuous experimentation. Real estate marketing is dynamic, and what works today may evolve over time. Regularly experiment with new ideas and approaches to stay ahead of market trends.

In conclusion, A/B testing and data analytics are powerful tools for real estate investors seeking to optimize listing performance. By strategically experimenting with different listing elements and leveraging data-driven insights, professionals can refine their approach, enhance user engagement, and ultimately drive successful real estate transactions. The iterative refinement process, informed by ongoing testing and analysis, ensures that property listings remain effective in capturing the attention of potential buyers or tenants in a competitive market.

Chapter 8: Effective Communication Strategies

Section 1: Building Rapport with Clients

Building rapport with clients is a fundamental aspect of successful real estate marketing. In this section, we explore the key elements of building strong relationships, focusing on establishing trust and credibility as the foundation. Additionally, we delve into effective communication techniques to foster positive client interactions.

A Establishing Trust and Credibility

1. The Foundational Importance of Trust in Client Relationships

Trust is the cornerstone of any successful client-professional relationship, especially in the realm of real estate. Clients entrust real estate investors with significant decisions, making it imperative to cultivate a sense of trust. Key considerations in establishing trust include:

- **Transparency and Honesty:** Transparent communication is crucial for building trust. Real estate investors should be upfront and honest with clients about market conditions, property details, and potential challenges. Openness fosters a sense of reliability and integrity.

- **Consistency and Reliability:** Consistent and reliable actions reinforce trust. Meeting commitments, adhering to timelines, and delivering on promises demonstrate professionalism and dedication to client satisfaction.

- **Client-Centric Approach:** Prioritize the client's best interests. Understanding their needs, preferences, and concerns demonstrates a commitment to serving their unique requirements, reinforcing trust in the professional-client relationship.

2. Building Credibility Through Transparent Communication and Reliability

Credibility is an extension of trust and is built through consistent and reliable communication. Real estate investors can enhance credibility by:

- **Providing Accurate Information:** Offering accurate and reliable information builds credibility. Misleading or inaccurate information can erode trust, emphasizing the importance of thorough research and verification.

- **Professional Expertise:** Demonstrating expertise as a real estate investor enhances credibility. Professionals should stay informed about industry trends, market conditions, and legal requirements to provide informed advice to clients.

- **Client Testimonials and References:** Leveraging positive client testimonials and references reinforces credibility. Sharing success stories and experiences from previous clients adds a layer of authenticity to a real estate investor's reputation.

B. Effective Communication Techniques

1. Strategies for Clear and Concise Communication

Clear and concise communication is essential for conveying information effectively and avoiding misunderstandings. Strategies for achieving clear communication include:

- **Use of Plain Language:** Avoid jargon or overly complex terminology. Use plain language that clients can easily understand, ensuring that communication is accessible and transparent.

- **Visual Aids and Presentations:** Supplement verbal communication with visual aids, such as charts, graphs, or presentations. Visual elements enhance comprehension and retention of important information.

- **Regular Updates:** Keep clients informed with regular updates. Whether it's market updates, progress reports on property transactions, or general communication, consistent updates contribute to a positive client experience.

2. Active Listening and Empathy in Client Interactions

Active listening and empathy are crucial components of effective communication. Real estate investors can employ the following techniques:

- **Active Listening Skills:** Actively listen to client concerns, questions, and preferences. Avoid interrupting and ensure that clients feel heard and understood. Repeating key points or summarizing discussions can demonstrate active listening.

- **Empathetic Understanding:** Empathy involves understanding and sharing the feelings of others. Real estate investors can build rapport by acknowledging and validating clients' emotions, demonstrating genuine care and concern.

- **Addressing Concerns and Questions:** Proactively address client concerns and questions. A responsive and attentive approach reinforces the client's importance and contributes to a positive client experience.

In conclusion, effective communication strategies are pivotal in real estate marketing, and building rapport with clients is a dynamic process that relies on trust, credibility, and clear communication. Establishing trust involves transparent and honest interactions, while credibility is built through consistent and reliable communication. Real estate investors must prioritize client-centric approaches, leveraging a client's best interests, and providing accurate information. Effective communication techniques, including clear and concise communication, active listening, and empathy, contribute to positive client interactions.

Section 2: Client Segmentation

Effective real estate marketing recognizes that one size does not fit all. This section explores the significance of tailoring communication to different client segments, emphasizing the understanding of diverse client personas and preferences. It delves into crafting messages that resonate with specific client demographics, personalizing marketing materials, and creating targeted campaigns based on client segmentation.

A. Tailoring Communication to Different Client Segments

1. Understanding Diverse Client Personas and Communication Preferences

As touched on earlier, real estate clients are a diverse group with varying needs, preferences, and communication styles. Tailoring communication involves gaining a deep understanding of different client personas:

- **Demographic Considerations:** Age, income, occupation, and lifestyle choices greatly influence how clients prefer to receive information. Millennials may prefer digital communication, while older generations might appreciate traditional methods.

- **Cultural Sensitivity:** Cultural nuances play a significant role. Understanding and respecting cultural differences help in crafting messages that resonate positively.

- **Communication Channels:** Some clients prefer emails, while others may respond better to phone calls or in-person meetings. Recognizing these preferences is key to effective communication.

- **Stage of Life:** Clients at different life stages have distinct needs. Families may prioritize spacious properties and proximity to schools, while young professionals might look for urban amenities.

- **Crafting Messages that Resonate:**

    - *Emphasizing Relevant Benefits:* Tailor messages to highlight how a property or service aligns with the specific needs and desires of the target segment. For instance, families may value safety and schools, while singles may prioritize proximity to nightlife.

- *Language and Tone:* Adjusting the language and tone of communication is crucial. Formality might be appreciated by certain segments, while others may respond better to a more casual approach.

- *Showcasing Shared Values:* Identify shared values between your brand and the client segment. If sustainability is essential to a particular demographic, emphasize eco-friendly features of properties.

B. Customizing Marketing Messages

1. Personalizing Marketing Materials for Segmented Audiences

- **Data-Driven Personalization:** Leverage data to personalize marketing materials. Use client information to address them by name, showcase properties that align with their preferences, and recommend relevant services.

- **Segment-Specific Content:** Create content that directly addresses the interests and concerns of specific segments. For example, create guides for first-time homebuyers or investment strategies for experienced clients.

- **Visual Appeal:** Tailor visuals to resonate with the aesthetics preferred by different segments. Images and graphics should evoke a positive emotional response aligned with the target audience.

2. Creating Targeted Campaigns Based on Client Segmentation

- **Segment-Specific Campaigns:** Instead of generic campaigns, design initiatives that specifically target different segments. This could involve hosting events, creating social media campaigns, or sending newsletters tailored to each group.

- **Personalized Offers:** Consider offering personalized incentives based on the segment. This could be exclusive discounts, additional services, or bundled packages that cater to the specific needs of each client group.

- **Feedback Loops:** Establish feedback mechanisms to continuously refine and optimize targeted campaigns. Client feedback provides valuable insights into the effectiveness of your strategies.

Case Studies

Example 1: Segment-Specific Open House Events

A real estate agency organized open house events tailored to different segments. For families, events highlighted nearby schools and safety features, while events for young professionals focused on urban amenities and connectivity.

Example 2: Personalized Digital Marketing Campaigns

Utilizing data analytics, an agency launched digital campaigns that personalized content based on client preferences. This resulted in higher engagement and increased lead conversions.

In conclusion, tailoring communication to diverse client segments is not just a strategy; it's a necessity in the dynamic landscape of real estate marketing. Understanding the unique needs, preferences, and lifestyles of different client personas enables real estate investors to build stronger connections, foster trust, and deliver value. Moving forward, the next section will delve into managing client expectations, a critical aspect of maintaining positive client relationships.

Section 3: Feedback and Improvement**

Feedback is the lifeblood of any successful real estate professional-client relationship. This section explores the importance of gathering and utilizing client feedback, emphasizing its role in understanding client satisfaction and implementing continuous improvement in communication and marketing strategies.

A. Gathering and Utilizing Client Feedback

1. Importance of Feedback in Understanding Client Satisfaction

Understanding the level of client satisfaction is essential for real estate investors seeking to provide excellent service and build lasting relationships. Here's why client feedback matters:

- **Insight into Client Experience:** Client feedback offers valuable insights into their overall experience. This includes their perception of your communication style, responsiveness, and the effectiveness of your guidance.

- **Identification of Strengths and Areas for Improvement:** Feedback helps identify your strengths, allowing you to reinforce successful strategies. Simultaneously, it highlights areas for improvement, guiding your efforts to enhance aspects of your service that may not meet client expectations.

- **Building Trust and Credibility:** Actively seeking feedback demonstrates a commitment to continuous improvement and client satisfaction. This dedication contributes to building trust and credibility, essential elements in the real estate industry.

- **Enhanced Client Retention:** Satisfied clients are more likely to become repeat clients or refer your services to others. By gathering feedback and addressing concerns, you contribute to positive experiences and enhance client retention.

2. Implementing Feedback Loops for Continuous Improvement

To create an effective feedback loop, real estate investors can employ several strategies:

- **Surveys and Questionnaires:** Utilize surveys or questionnaires to gather structured feedback. These tools can cover specific aspects of the real estate process, such as property search, negotiation, or transaction management.

- **Regular Check-Ins:** Incorporate regular check-ins during and after transactions to solicit feedback. These can be in the form of casual conversations, ensuring clients feel comfortable sharing their thoughts.

- **Online Reviews and Testimonials:** Encourage clients to leave online reviews and testimonials. Positive reviews not only boost your online reputation but also serve as public endorsements of your services.

- **Feedback Meetings:** Schedule dedicated feedback meetings where clients can express their thoughts in a face-to-face setting. This personal interaction fosters open communication.

B. Continuous Improvement in Communication Strategies

1. The Role of Feedback in Refining Communication Approaches

Effective communication is dynamic and should evolve based on client needs and industry trends. Client feedback plays a pivotal role in refining communication approaches by:

- **Identifying Preferred Communication Channels:** Clients may have preferences for specific communication channels. Feedback helps you identify these preferences, ensuring you use the channels most comfortable and convenient for your clients.

- **Adjusting Tone and Style:** Feedback provides insights into how clients perceive your communication tone and style. Use this information to tailor your approach to better match the expectations and preferences of different clients.

- **Enhancing Responsiveness:** Timely responsiveness is a key aspect of effective communication. Client feedback can highlight areas where improvements in response times are needed, leading to more efficient communication.

- **Clarifying Information Delivery:** Different clients have varying preferences for the level of detail in information delivery. Feedback helps you understand whether clients prefer concise overviews or more comprehensive explanations, allowing you to adjust accordingly.

2. Iterative Enhancement of Communication Strategies Based on Feedback

The process of continuous improvement is iterative and ongoing. Real estate investors can follow a structured approach to enhance communication strategies based on feedback:

- **Regular Review Sessions:** Schedule regular review sessions to analyze client feedback. This could be a monthly or quarterly practice to ensure continuous monitoring and adjustment.

- **Team Collaboration:** If working within a team, collaborate with colleagues to share feedback and collectively identify areas for improvement. A team-based approach fosters a culture of continuous learning.

- **Professional Development:** Invest in professional development opportunities to enhance communication skills. This could include workshops, training sessions, or industry conferences that focus on effective client communication.

- **Technology Integration:** Explore technological tools that can enhance communication efficiency. This may include adopting communication platforms that facilitate seamless interactions and provide a better client experience.

In conclusion, the synergy between gathering and utilizing client feedback and continuous improvement in communication strategies is essential for real estate investors aiming for excellence. By actively seeking feedback, understanding client satisfaction, and iteratively refining communication approaches, investors can build stronger client relationships and elevate their service delivery. The next section will explore strategies for effective crisis communication, a crucial skill in navigating unexpected challenges in the real estate industry.

Chapter 9: Financial Management in Real Estate Marketing

Section 1: Budgeting for Marketing Campaigns

Marketing is a crucial component of a successful real estate investment strategy, and effective budgeting ensures that resources are allocated wisely to achieve optimal results. This section explores strategies for allocating resources across diverse marketing channels and implementing cost-effective approaches.

A. Allocating Resources for Different Marketing Channels

1. Understanding the Importance of Channel Allocation

In the diverse landscape of real estate marketing, allocating resources effectively is akin to distributing your artillery strategically on a battlefield. Each marketing channel serves a unique purpose, and understanding how to allocate resources ensures a comprehensive and targeted approach. Strategies for effective channel allocation include:

- **Identifying High-Impact Channels:** Evaluate the performance and reach of various marketing channels. This includes digital channels such as social media, search engine optimization (SEO), and email marketing, as well as traditional channels like direct mail and networking events.

- **Aligning Channels with Goals:** Align channel selection with your marketing goals. If brand awareness is a priority, social media and content marketing may be emphasized. If lead generation is the focus, targeted online advertising and SEO may take precedence.

- **Consideration of Target Audience:** Different demographics and segments may respond differently to various channels. Tailor your channel allocation to reach your specific target audience effectively. For example, younger demographics might be more responsive to social media, while older demographics may prefer traditional methods.

- **Budget Flexibility:** Maintain flexibility in your budget allocation to adapt to changing market conditions. Regularly assess the performance of each channel and be prepared to reallocate resources based on evolving marketing needs.

B Cost-Effective Strategies

1. Exploring Cost-Effective Marketing Approaches

Real estate marketing doesn't always require exorbitant budgets. Cost-effective strategies can deliver significant results without breaking the bank. Here are strategies to explore:

- **Content Marketing on a Budget:** Invest time and effort in creating valuable content without heavy financial expenses. Blogging, creating informative videos, and offering downloadable resources can establish your expertise without significant monetary outlays.

- **Social Media Engagement:** Leverage the power of social media without a hefty budget. Consistent and engaging content, strategic use of hashtags, and participation in relevant discussions can boost your online presence organically.

- **DIY Graphic Design:** Platforms like Canva provide user-friendly tools for creating professional-looking graphics. Instead of outsourcing design work, you can create eye-catching visuals for social media, blogs, and other marketing materials.

- **Networking Events on a Budget:** Attend local networking events that may have lower participation costs. Additionally, consider hosting smaller, targeted events that showcase your expertise and allow for meaningful connections without extravagant expenses.

2. Maximizing Results Within Budget Constraints

A constrained budget doesn't mean compromising on results; it requires strategic planning and maximizing the impact of each allocated dollar. Consider the following approaches:

- **Focus on High-ROI Channels:** Identify channels that consistently deliver a high return on investment (ROI). Allocate a larger proportion of your budget to these channels to ensure maximum impact.

- **Negotiate Advertising Costs:** When engaging in paid advertising, negotiate rates with publishers or platforms. Bulk purchases or long-term commitments may provide opportunities for cost savings.

- **Prioritize Data Analysis:** Invest in analytics tools to track the performance of your marketing campaigns. Regularly analyze data to identify what is working and where adjustments can be made to optimize results.

- **Collaborate and Cross-Promote:** Forge partnerships with other businesses or professionals in the industry. Collaborative efforts, such as joint events or cross-promotions, can extend your reach without additional financial burdens.

In conclusion, effective budgeting is a cornerstone of financial management in real estate marketing. By strategically allocating resources across diverse channels and implementing cost-effective strategies, real estate investors can maximize their impact and achieve their marketing goals within budget constraints.

Section 2: ROI Analysis

ROI (Return on Investment) is a critical metric in real estate marketing, providing insights into the effectiveness of campaigns and guiding strategic decision-making. This section explores methods for measuring ROI in real estate marketing, establishing benchmarks for success, and how to adjust strategies based on performance.

A. Measuring the Return on Investment for Marketing Efforts

1. Understanding ROI in Real Estate Marketing

ROI is a key performance indicator that assesses the profitability of an investment relative to its cost. In real estate marketing, where resources are allocated across various channels, measuring ROI provides valuable insights into which strategies are yielding the best results. Methods for calculating ROI include:

- **Campaign-Specific ROI Calculation:** Break down the investment and returns for each marketing campaign. Calculate the net gain from a campaign by subtracting the cost from the revenue generated as a direct result of that specific initiative.

- **Customer Lifetime Value (CLV):** Consider the long-term value of acquired customers. Calculate the CLV by estimating the total revenue a customer is expected to generate over their entire relationship with the business, factoring in repeat transactions and referrals.

- **Attribution Modeling:** Use attribution models to assign value to different touchpoints in a customer's journey. This helps understand the contribution of each marketing channel or campaign to the overall conversion.

- **Cost per Acquisition (CPA):** Determine the cost of acquiring a new customer. Divide the total costs associated with a specific marketing campaign by the number of new customers generated through that campaign.

2. Establishing Benchmarks for Successful ROI

- **Industry Averages:** Research industry benchmarks to understand average ROI figures for real estate marketing. This provides a baseline for comparison and helps evaluate whether your campaigns are performing above or below industry standards.

- **Historical Performance:** Analyze the ROI of past campaigns to establish internal benchmarks. Understanding what has worked well in the past allows for the identification of successful strategies to replicate and build upon.

- **Competitor Analysis:** Study the ROI performance of competitors. While exact figures may not be available, understanding the general success of competitor marketing efforts can help gauge your standing in the market.

B. Adjusting Strategies Based on Performance

1. Utilizing ROI Data to Refine and Optimize Marketing Strategies

- **Identifying High-Performing Channels:** Analyze the ROI data to identify channels or campaigns that consistently deliver strong results. Allocate more resources to these high-performing areas to maximize returns.

- **Eliminating or Adjusting Underperforming Elements:** Pinpoint underperforming campaigns or channels and assess whether adjustments can be made to improve their effectiveness. If certain strategies consistently yield poor ROI, consider reallocating resources to more promising opportunities.

- **Iterative Improvements for Enhanced Performance and Efficiency:** Approach marketing as an iterative process. Use ROI data to inform ongoing improvements. Test new strategies, measure their impact on ROI, and refine approaches based on continuous learning.

2. Adapting Strategies to Market Dynamics

- **Market Changes:** Keep an eye on market dynamics and adjust strategies accordingly. External factors, such as changes in consumer behavior or economic conditions, may require adaptations to maintain optimal ROI.

- **Technological Advancements:** Stay abreast of technological advancements that can enhance marketing efficiency. Embrace new tools or platforms that align with evolving consumer preferences and improve ROI.

- **Feedback from Clients and Customers:** Customer feedback can provide valuable insights into the effectiveness of marketing efforts. Use feedback to refine messaging, targeting, and overall strategy to better meet customer expectations.

In conclusion, ROI analysis is a dynamic process that requires continuous monitoring, assessment, and adaptation. By employing various methods to calculate ROI, establishing benchmarks, and adjusting strategies based on performance data, real estate investors can ensure that their marketing efforts are not only cost-effective but also optimized for success.

Section 3: Scaling Successful Campaigns

Scaling successful marketing campaigns is a crucial aspect of financial management in real estate marketing. This section explores the indicators of successful campaigns, strategies for expansion, and the delicate balance between scalability and resource constraints.

A. Expanding Successful Marketing Initiatives

1. Identifying Indicators of Successful Campaigns

- **Conversion Rates:** A high conversion rate indicates that the campaign resonates with the target audience and effectively prompts them to take desired actions, whether it's making a purchase, scheduling a consultation, or signing up for newsletters.

- **Lead Generation:** Successful campaigns generate a substantial number of qualified leads. If a campaign consistently attracts leads that convert into clients, it's a strong indicator of success.

- **Return on Investment (ROI):** As discussed in the previous section, analyzing the ROI of a campaign is crucial. A positive ROI suggests that the campaign is generating more revenue than the costs incurred, making it a viable candidate for scaling.

- **Audience Engagement:** Monitoring audience engagement through metrics such as click-through rates, social media interactions, and content shares provides insights into how well the campaign resonates with the audience.

- **Brand Visibility and Recognition:** Successful campaigns enhance brand visibility and recognition. An increase in brand mentions, positive reviews, and a growing social media following are signs that a campaign is making a positive impact.

2. Strategies for Scaling Successful Campaigns to Reach a Broader Audience

- **Replicating Successful Tactics:** Identify the specific elements or tactics that contributed to the success of the campaign. Replicate these successful components in new initiatives to maintain the winning formula.

- **Expanding Target Audience:** Evaluate the potential to expand the target audience without diluting the effectiveness of the campaign. This may involve targeting new demographics or geographic areas that align with the campaign's objectives.

- **Multi-Channel Integration:** Explore opportunities to integrate successful campaigns across multiple channels. For example, if a digital campaign performs well, consider adapting elements for offline channels or vice versa.

- **Localized Adaptations:** Customize successful campaigns for different local markets. Tailoring messaging and visuals to resonate with specific regional characteristics can enhance effectiveness in diverse locations.

B. Balancing Scalability with Resource Constraints

1. Evaluating Scalability Options While Considering Budget and Resource Limitations

- **Incremental Expansion:** Instead of making drastic changes, consider incremental expansion. Gradual scaling allows for better control and assessment of the impact on resources.

- **Technology and Automation:** Leverage technology and automation to scale without a proportional increase in labor or operational costs.

Marketing automation tools can streamline processes and manage larger audiences efficiently.

- **Collaborations and Partnerships:** Explore collaborations or partnerships that can help amplify the reach of the campaign without significantly increasing the budget. Joint ventures with complementary businesses or influencers can provide access to new audiences.

2. Efficient Scaling to Maximize Impact Without Overspending

- **Budget Allocation:** Allocate resources judiciously by prioritizing high-impact activities. Identify areas where additional investment can yield substantial returns and focus resources on those aspects.

- **Performance Monitoring:** Implement robust monitoring mechanisms to track the performance of scaled initiatives. Regularly assess key performance indicators to ensure that scaling efforts are aligned with the desired outcomes.

- **Feedback and Iterative Improvement:** Solicit feedback from the expanded audience and use it to iteratively improve the campaign. Continuous refinement based on real-time data ensures that scaling efforts are adaptive and responsive to audience needs.

In conclusion, scaling successful marketing campaigns in real estate requires a strategic approach that balances expansion with resource constraints. By identifying indicators of success, replicating effective tactics, and carefully evaluating scalability options, real estate investors can maximize the impact of their campaigns while maintaining financial efficiency.

Section 4: Risk Management in Marketing

Effective risk management is a critical component of financial stewardship in real estate marketing. This section explores the proactive identification of marketing risks, strategies for mitigating these risks, and the importance of contingency planning to navigate unforeseen challenges.

A. Identifying and Mitigating Marketing Risks

Market Volatility

Real estate markets can be subject to volatility due to economic fluctuations, regulatory changes, or unexpected events. Mitigation strategies involve diversifying marketing channels to reduce reliance on a single source and staying informed about market trends.

Reputation Risks

Negative publicity, customer dissatisfaction, or unfavorable reviews can damage a real estate professional's reputation. Establishing robust customer service protocols, actively addressing concerns, and fostering positive client relationships can mitigate these risks.

Regulatory Compliance

Real estate marketing must adhere to various regulations. Non-compliance can result in legal consequences. Regularly updating marketing practices based on legal requirements and seeking legal advice when needed are crucial risk mitigation steps.

Technological Risks

Dependence on technology exposes real estate investors to risks such as data breaches and system failures. Implementing cybersecurity measures, regular software updates, and data backup protocols help safeguard against technological risks.

Competitive Pressures

Intense competition is inherent in the real estate industry. Identifying unique selling propositions and continuously monitoring competitors' strategies can help real estate investors differentiate themselves and mitigate competitive pressures.

B. Contingency Planning for Unforeseen Challenges

Preparing for Unexpected Challenges Through Contingency Planning

Contingency planning involves foreseeing potential challenges and preparing response strategies. Real estate investors should conduct a thorough risk assessment to identify plausible scenarios that could impact marketing efforts.

Maintaining Flexibility in Marketing Strategies to Adapt to Changing Circumstances

Flexibility is key to effective contingency planning. Real estate marketing strategies should be adaptable, allowing for swift adjustments in response to unforeseen challenges. This flexibility ensures that campaigns remain resilient in dynamic environments.

Scenario Analysis

Real estate investors can conduct scenario analyses to simulate various market conditions and assess the impact on marketing strategies. This helps in identifying potential risks and developing corresponding contingency plans.

Establishing Communication Protocols

Contingency planning should include well-defined communication protocols. In the event of a crisis or unforeseen challenge, clear communication internally and externally is crucial for managing perceptions and maintaining trust.

Financial Reserves

Building financial reserves provides a safety net during challenging times. Allocating a portion of the marketing budget to a contingency fund ensures that there are resources available to address unexpected challenges without compromising ongoing initiatives.

In conclusion, risk management is integral to the financial health of real estate marketing efforts. By proactively identifying potential risks, implementing mitigation strategies, and developing contingency plans, real estate investors can navigate challenges and maintain the resilience of their marketing campaigns.

Section 5: Financial Planning for Long-Term Success

Effective financial planning is paramount for the sustained success of real estate marketing endeavors. This section explores the development of a sustainable financial plan for marketing activities, emphasizing the importance of balancing short-term gains with long-term stability. Additionally, it delves into long-term growth strategies and the necessity of adapting financial plans to accommodate evolving market dynamics.

A. Creating a Sustainable Financial Plan for Marketing Activities

Aligning Financial Plans with Marketing Goals

A cohesive alignment between financial plans and marketing goals is crucial for success. Real estate investors must clearly define their marketing objectives and allocate resources accordingly to achieve a positive return on investment.

Budget Allocation for Diverse Marketing Channels

A sustainable financial plan involves judiciously allocating budgets across diverse marketing channels. While digital marketing may yield immediate results, traditional methods may contribute to long-term brand building. Striking the right balance is essential.

Investing in Talent and Training

Building a successful marketing team requires investment in talent acquisition and ongoing training. A well-trained and motivated team contributes to the effectiveness of marketing campaigns and fosters a culture of innovation and adaptability.

Technology Investments

Staying abreast of technological advancements is essential for real estate marketing. Allocating resources for adopting and integrating new technologies ensures a competitive edge and enhances efficiency in marketing processes.

Monitoring and Adjusting Financial Plans

Real estate markets are dynamic, and financial plans must be flexible. Regular monitoring and adjustments to financial strategies in response to market shifts and campaign performance are crucial for maintaining relevance and effectiveness.

B. Long-Term Growth Strategies

Diversification of Marketing Strategies

Long-term success necessitates a diversified approach to marketing. Real estate investors should explore new strategies and adapt to emerging trends while maintaining core marketing practices that have proven successful.

Brand Building for Market Authority

Building a strong brand contributes to long-term success by establishing market authority. Consistent brand messaging, quality service delivery, and community engagement foster trust, making the brand synonymous with reliability and expertise.

Customer Relationship Management (CRM)

Investing in a CRM system for effective client management and communication is integral to long-term success. Maintaining strong relationships with past clients can lead to repeat business and referrals, contributing to sustained growth.

Adapting to Market Trends

Staying attuned to market trends is critical for long-term success. Real estate investors should continually assess market dynamics, consumer preferences, and industry innovations to adapt their marketing strategies accordingly.

Strategic Partnerships and Collaborations

Forming strategic partnerships with other businesses and professionals in the real estate ecosystem fosters mutual growth. Collaborative marketing efforts, cross-promotions, and shared initiatives contribute to expanding reach and influence.

In conclusion, the financial planning for long-term success in real estate marketing involves a delicate balance between short-term gains and sustained stability. By aligning financial plans with marketing goals, diversifying strategies, and adapting to market trends, real estate investors can position themselves for enduring success.

Chapter 10: Adapting to Market Changes & Summary

Section 1: Monitoring Market Trends

Adaptability is a cornerstone of success in real estate marketing, and staying informed about industry shifts is crucial for navigating the dynamic landscape. This section explores the significance of staying current with real estate market trends and offers insights into adapting marketing strategies accordingly.

A. Staying Informed About Industry Shifts

Understanding the Dynamic Nature of Real Estate

The real estate industry is inherently dynamic, with trends, consumer preferences, and market conditions constantly evolving. Real estate investors must recognize that staying informed is not just a task but an ongoing commitment to excellence.

Utilizing Resources and Tools for Continuous Monitoring

Embracing technology and leveraging industry resources is essential for continuous monitoring. Subscribing to real estate publications, attending industry conferences, and utilizing market research tools help professionals stay ahead of emerging trends.

Networking and Collaboration

Networking with industry peers and professionals provides valuable insights into market dynamics. Collaborative discussions, sharing experiences, and participating in forums contribute to a collective understanding of ongoing shifts in the real estate landscape.

Data-Driven Decision Making

Harnessing the power of data is integral to staying informed. Real estate investors should employ analytics tools to interpret market data, identify patterns, and make informed decisions based on quantitative insights.

2. Adapting Marketing Strategies Accordingly

Strategies for Adjusting Marketing Plans Based on Emerging Trends

Recognizing emerging trends is only valuable if coupled with proactive adjustments to marketing plans. Whether it's a shift in consumer behavior, technological advancements, or regulatory changes, adapting strategies promptly is crucial.

Leveraging Market Shifts as Opportunities for Innovation

Rather than viewing market shifts as challenges, successful real estate investors see them as opportunities for innovation. Adapting marketing strategies to align with emerging trends positions professionals as forward-thinking and responsive to client needs.

Agility and Flexibility in Campaign Execution

Marketing campaigns should be designed with flexibility in mind. Agile execution allows for quick adjustments based on real-time feedback, ensuring that marketing efforts are always aligned with the most current market dynamics.

Customer-Centric Approach

An effective response to market trends involves a customer-centric approach. Understanding changing customer needs and preferences allows for the tailoring of marketing messages and services to align with what resonates most with the target audience.

Embracing Sustainable Practices

In an era of increasing environmental awareness, adapting marketing strategies may involve embracing sustainable practices. From eco-friendly property development to green marketing campaigns, aligning with sustainability trends can attract environmentally conscious clients.

In conclusioin, in the ever-evolving landscape of real estate, monitoring market trends and adapting marketing strategies accordingly is not just a best practice but a fundamental necessity. The ability to stay ahead of industry shifts, leverage emerging opportunities, and swiftly adjust strategies positions real estate investors for sustained success.

Section 2: Regulatory Changes in Real Estate

The real estate industry operates within a framework of regulations and legal considerations that can significantly impact marketing practices. This section explores the impact of regulatory changes on real estate marketing and provides strategies for staying compliant while navigating legal challenges.

A. Understanding and Complying with Regulatory Updates

The Dynamics of Regulatory Changes

Real estate is subject to various regulations that can change over time. These changes may stem from shifts in local, state, or federal laws, and they often have a direct impact on how professionals can market properties and communicate with clients.

The Impact of Regulatory Changes on Real Estate Marketing

Regulatory updates can influence advertising guidelines, disclosure requirements, fair housing laws, and more. It is crucial for real estate investors to understand the implications of these changes on marketing strategies to avoid legal complications.

Strategies for Staying Compliant

Professionals must establish robust mechanisms for staying informed about regulatory updates. This involves regular training, subscribing to legal updates, and maintaining open communication with legal counsel to ensure all marketing practices align with current regulations.

Adapting Marketing Practices

Understanding the specific changes in regulations allows for the adaptation of marketing practices. For instance, if there are new restrictions on certain advertising claims or methods, marketing materials can be adjusted to ensure compliance.

B. Navigating Legal Challenges in Marketing

Identifying Potential Legal Challenges

Real estate marketing can encounter legal challenges related to misrepresentation, non-disclosure, or violations of fair housing laws. Identifying potential legal pitfalls beforehand enables professionals to proactively address issues.

Establishing Protocols for Navigating Legal Issues

Having clear protocols in place for addressing legal challenges is essential. This involves creating a system for reviewing marketing materials, ensuring accurate property representations, and promptly addressing any legal concerns that arise.

Legal Compliance Training

Providing ongoing legal compliance training for real estate investors is crucial. This education ensures that team members are well-versed in the legal landscape, reducing the likelihood of inadvertent violations.

Collaboration with Legal Professionals

Establishing a collaborative relationship with legal professionals specializing in real estate ensures that marketing practices align with legal requirements. Legal counsel can provide insights, review marketing materials, and offer guidance on potential risks.

Ethical Considerations

Beyond legal obligations, ethical considerations should also guide marketing practices. This includes transparent communication, honesty in advertising, and a commitment to fair and non-discriminatory practices.

In conclusdion, adapting to regulatory changes and navigating legal challenges is a fundamental aspect of real estate marketing. By staying informed, proactively adjusting strategies, and establishing protocols for legal compliance, professionals can ensure that their marketing efforts not only attract clients but also withstand legal scrutiny.

Section 3: Technological Advances and Innovations

In the ever-evolving landscape of real estate marketing, embracing new technologies is not just a choice but a necessity for staying competitive. This section explores the role of emerging technologies and the importance of continuous learning and adaptation in the realm of real estate marketing.

A. Embracing New Technologies for Marketing

The Dynamics of Real Estate Technology

As previously discussed, the real estate industry has witnessed a rapid influx of technological innovations, reshaping the way properties are marketed and transactions are conducted. From artificial intelligence (AI) to virtual reality (VR) and blockchain, these technologies have the potential to revolutionize marketing strategies.

Exploring the Role of Emerging Technologies

- *Artificial Intelligence (AI):* AI applications in real estate include predictive analytics for market trends, chatbots for customer interactions, and machine learning algorithms for personalized marketing campaigns.

- *Virtual Reality (VR):* VR enables immersive property presentations through virtual tours, allowing potential buyers to experience properties remotely. This technology enhances the visualization of spaces and can significantly impact decision-making.

- *Blockchain:* Blockchain technology can enhance security and transparency in real estate transactions. Its decentralized nature ensures that property data is secure and unalterable, reducing the risk of fraud.

Integrating Innovative Tools

Real estate investors need to actively integrate these innovative tools into their marketing strategies. This involves leveraging AI for data-driven decision-making, incorporating VR in property presentations, and exploring blockchain applications for secure transactions.

Enhancing Customer Experience

The adoption of these technologies is not just about staying current; it's about providing a superior customer experience. Virtual property tours, AI-driven property recommendations, and blockchain-secured transactions contribute to a more efficient and secure real estate journey for clients.

B. Continuous Learning and Adaptation

Strategies for Ongoing Education

- *Professional Development Courses:* Real estate investors should engage in ongoing education courses that focus on the latest technologies. These courses can be industry-specific or cover broader technological trends.

- *Technology Workshops and Seminars:* Attending workshops and seminars dedicated to real estate technology provides hands-on experience and insights from experts. These events facilitate networking and knowledge exchange.

- *Online Resources and Webinars:* The internet is a treasure trove of information on emerging technologies. Webinars, online courses, and industry forums offer a convenient way to stay updated and learn at one's own pace.

Fostering a Culture of Adaptability

- *Leadership Initiatives:* Leadership within real estate firms plays a crucial role in fostering a culture of adaptability. Encouraging team members to embrace new technologies requires leadership support and initiatives.

- *Collaborative Learning Environment:* Establishing a collaborative learning environment where team members can share insights, discoveries, and challenges related to technology creates a collective knowledge pool.

- *Experimentation and Innovation:* Encouraging a culture of experimentation allows professionals to test and implement new technologies. Innovation often arises from a willingness to try new approaches and learn from both successes and failures.

In conclusion, embracing technological advances in real estate marketing is not just a matter of survival; it's an opportunity for growth and innovation. By exploring and integrating emerging technologies, coupled with a commitment to continuous learning, real estate investors can position themselves as industry leaders, offering clients a cutting-edge and seamless experience.

Section 4: Economic Influences on Real Estate Marketing

Real estate marketing does not exist in isolation; it is deeply intertwined with the broader economic landscape. This section delves into the crucial aspect of economic influences on real estate marketing, emphasizing the importance of analyzing economic factors and adjusting strategies in response to changes in the market.

A. Analyzing Economic Factors Affecting the Market

Understanding Economic Dynamics

Real estate is profoundly affected by the economic environment. Various economic factors play a pivotal role in shaping the demand and supply dynamics of the real estate market. These include:

- *Interest Rates:* Fluctuations in interest rates can impact borrowing costs, influencing both homebuyers and property investors.

- *Employment Trends:* Employment rates and income levels directly affect the ability of individuals to enter the housing market.

- *Inflation Rates:* Inflation can influence property values, impacting both residential and commercial real estate.

- *Consumer Confidence:* The overall sentiment and confidence levels of consumers can affect their willingness to engage in real estate transactions.

Monitoring Indicators for Potential Market Changes

Real estate investors need to be vigilant in monitoring economic indicators. This involves staying informed about:

- *GDP Growth:* The overall economic health, as measured by Gross Domestic Product (GDP), provides insights into the strength of the real estate market.

- *Housing Starts:* The number of new housing construction projects can indicate the direction of the real estate market.

- *Unemployment Rates:* Fluctuations in employment rates can signal shifts in demand for housing.

B. Adjusting Marketing Strategies in Response to Economic Changes

Strategies for Adapting Marketing Approaches

- *Flexible Campaigns:* Real estate marketing plans should incorporate flexibility to adjust to economic changes. This involves having multiple campaign strategies that can be activated based on the prevailing economic conditions.

- *Targeted Marketing:* During economic downturns, targeted marketing efforts may focus on cost-effective channels and emphasize value propositions. During economic upswings, there may be opportunities to expand marketing efforts.

- *Messaging Adjustments:* The messaging in marketing materials should align with the economic climate. In challenging times, messages may emphasize stability and value, while in prosperous times, they may highlight opportunities and growth.

Ensuring Marketing Plans Align with the Economic Climate

- *Regular Strategy Reviews:* Real estate investors should conduct regular reviews of marketing strategies to ensure alignment with the current economic climate. This includes reassessing target audiences, adjusting budgets, and refining messaging.

- *Scenario Planning:* Scenario planning involves developing strategies for different economic scenarios. By anticipating potential economic shifts, real estate investors can proactively adjust their marketing plans.

- *Collaboration with Economic Analysts:* Collaboration with economic analysts or consultants can provide valuable insights. These professionals can help interpret economic data and guide real estate marketing strategies accordingly.

In conclusion, the economic landscape is dynamic, and real estate marketing strategies must be dynamic in response. Analyzing economic factors and adjusting marketing strategies accordingly is not just a reactive approach; it's a strategic imperative for long-term success.

Section 5: Building a Resilient Marketing Strategy

In the ever-evolving landscape of real estate, a resilient marketing strategy is not just an advantage; it's a necessity. This section explores the critical elements of creating a flexible and resilient marketing plan, highlighting the importance of adaptability and learning from failures for sustained success.

A. Creating a Flexible and Resilient Marketing Plan

The Importance of Flexibility in Marketing Strategy

Flexibility is a cornerstone of a resilient marketing strategy. Real estate investors must recognize that market conditions, consumer behaviors, and external factors can change rapidly. Key components include:

- *Agility:* The ability to respond quickly and effectively to changing circumstances is a hallmark of a resilient marketing plan.

- *Scalability:* A plan should be scalable to accommodate both periods of growth and contraction in the real estate market.

Developing Contingency Plans for Unforeseen Circumstances

- *Risk Assessment:* Identifying potential risks and challenges is the first step. This includes considering economic downturns, regulatory changes, and unexpected crises.

- *Contingency Strategies:* Developing specific strategies to address identified risks ensures that the marketing plan can pivot when needed. These strategies may involve alternative channels, messaging adjustments, or budget reallocations.

B. Learning from Failures and Adapting for Future Success

Embracing Failures as Learning Opportunities

- *Shift in Perspective:* Rather than viewing failures as setbacks, a resilient marketing strategy sees them as opportunities for growth and improvement.

- *Case Analysis:* Real estate investors should conduct in-depth analyses of marketing campaigns that did not meet expectations. This involves identifying what went wrong, why it went wrong, and what lessons can be extracted.

Utilizing Lessons Learned to Refine and Strengthen Marketing Strategies

- *Iterative Improvement:* The process of continuous improvement is central to building resilience. Real estate investors should apply lessons learned from past failures to refine existing strategies.

- *Feedback Loops:* Establishing feedback loops within marketing campaigns ensures that insights from performance data are continuously integrated. This iterative approach allows for adjustments in real-time.

- *Adaptive Innovation:* A resilient marketing strategy is not afraid to innovate. It involves a culture of adaptive innovation, where new ideas are tested and integrated based on the evolving needs of the market.

Case Studies

- *Example 1: Economic Downturn:* During an economic downturn, a real estate firm faced challenges with its high-end luxury property marketing strategy. Learning from this, they pivoted to emphasize value and long-term investment benefits, successfully adapting to the economic climate.

- *Example 2: Regulatory Changes:* A real estate agency encountered unexpected regulatory changes impacting property transactions. By swiftly adjusting their marketing messaging to address concerns arising from the changes, they maintained client trust and continued operations effectively.

In conclusion, building a resilient marketing strategy in real estate requires a combination of foresight, adaptability, and a willingness to learn from both successes and failures. As the industry continues to evolve, those with resilient strategies will not only weather changes but emerge stronger and more prepared for the challenges and opportunities that lie ahead. This concludes our exploration of adapting to market changes in real estate marketing.

Conclusion

In conclusion, this comprehensive guide has navigated through the intricate landscape of real estate investing and marketing, providing a roadmap for success in an ever-evolving industry. The journey commenced with an exploration of the fundamental concepts, introducing real estate investing and underscoring the pivotal role marketing plays in shaping outcomes. The importance of understanding diverse real estate investments, assessing risks and rewards, and aligning goals with marketing strategies were dissected in the section on investment fundamentals. Moving forward, the guide meticulously examined the intricacies of marketing, emphasizing the competitive nature of the industry, the plethora of marketing strategies available, and the significance of client segmentation.

As we progressed through the chapters, the guide transitioned to the critical aspect of building a brand, dissecting the components of a brand identity and illuminating the power of a strong brand in attracting clients and partners. Targeting the right markets emerged as a pivotal strategy, delving into market research, understanding buyer and seller behavior, niche marketing, competitive analysis, and the importance of data-driven decision-making. The exploration of digital marketing strategies uncovered the vast realm of online advertising, content marketing, search engine optimization, email marketing, and social media marketing, demonstrating how these tools can be harnessed for effective outreach in the digital landscape.

The subsequent chapters delved into offline marketing strategies, leveraging technology, crafting compelling property listings, and honing effective communication strategies. Financial management in real estate marketing was explored comprehensively, covering budgeting, ROI analysis, scaling campaigns, risk management, and long-term financial planning. The guide rounded off with an insightful exploration of adapting to market changes, including monitoring market trends, navigating regulatory updates, embracing technological advances, understanding economic influences, and building a resilient marketing strategy.

Throughout this journey, real-world case studies, actionable insights, and strategic frameworks were unveiled to equip readers with the knowledge and tools needed to thrive in the dynamic realm of real estate investing and marketing. As the real estate landscape continues to evolve, this guide serves as a timeless companion, providing a robust foundation and adaptable strategies for success in the multifaceted world of real estate.

Good luck.

Check out WWW.JIMPELLERIN.COM[1] for more articles on Real Estate Investing.

1. http://WWW.JIMPELLERIN.COM

About The Author

JIM PELLERIN started real estate investing over twenty years ago. Since then, he has bought and sold millions of dollars of real estate. He began by purchasing and renting out duplexes. Recently he has added Lease Options to his strategy. He is currently acquiring two to four Lease Option properties a month. He has implemented many unique funding strategies that have allowed him to continue implementing his strategy and continue building his sizable portfolio.

As part of his education, he has attended numerous seminars on real estate investing, project management, property management, financing, renovations, motivation, time management, and many more. He has also read over 500 books on similar topics.

This book blends his experience and the knowledge he has gained through his investments and studies.

Visit his author page to discover my other publications: books2read.com/JimPellerin[1]

1. https://books2read.com/JimPellerin

Other Books By Jim Pellerin

Real Estate Investing: Strategies – The Secret to Financial Independence with Real Estate

books2read.com/strategies[1]

1. https://books2read.com/strategies

Real Estate Investing with Lease Options – How to Invest with No Money Down

books2read.com/Lease-Options[2]

2. https://books2read.com/Lease-Options

Invest NOW – The Passive Approach to Winning with Real Estate

books2read.com/investnow[3]

3. https://books2read.com/investnow

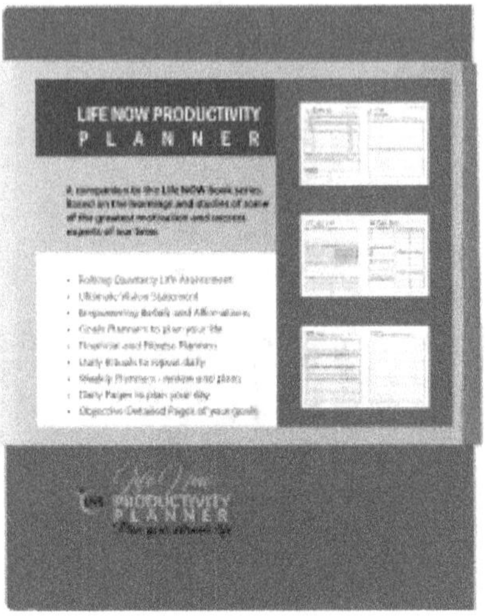

books2read.com/JimPellerin[4]

4. https://books2read.com/JimPellerin

Did you love *The Ultimate Guide to Marketing for Real Estate Investors*? Then you should read *Real Estate Investing Strategies: The Secret to Financial Independence with Real Estate*[5] by Jim Pellerin!

[6]

The mechanics of Real Estate Investing is simple: Buy a house and do something with it. Fix it and rent it, or just sell it. Sounds simple, doesn't it? Yet only a small percentage of us have enough courage to go out and take advantage of the opportunities that are available to us. Real Estate Investing can be more promising than stocks, bonds, and various other securities because of the higher rates of return.

In this book, I show you how to get started by describing the different types of skills you need, by showing you how to take control of your personal and financial situation, and by helping you decide what type of real estate investing you want to get involved in. I also show

5. https://books2read.com/u/m2QyNG

6. https://books2read.com/u/m2QyNG

you how to find properties, how to analyze them, and how to make an offer that makes sense. And finally, I describe what you need to do to manage your investment and ultimately how to sell your investment for the most profit.

I have been involved in real estate investing for over 20 years. I have yet to find a book that focuses on the investor and the overall process. Sure, there are lots of books on fix and flips, buy, rent and hold, rent to own, etc. However, I haven't found any good books on how to really get started in the real estate investing process from a practical viewpoint. The technical aspects of real estate investing are really quite easy. But if it's so easy, then why isn't everyone doing it?

This book is for people who are serious about getting started in real estate investing and who want to join the 5% of those who actually take action and invest. This book provides a strategic approach with the tried and tested methods and principles that have helped others make millions in real estate.

Read more at www.jimpellerin.com.

Also by Jim Pellerin

Real Estate Investing

Real Estate Investing Strategies: The Secret to Financial Independence with Real Estate

Real Estate Investing with Lease Options - Investing in Real Estate with No Money Down

Invest Now - The Passive Approach to Winning at Real Estate

The Ultimate Beginners Guide to Real Estate Investing

The 98 Best Real Estate Investing Strategies

The Ultimate Beginners Guide to Wholesale Real Estate Investing

The Ultimate Beginners Guide to Rental Real Estate Investing

The Ultimate Beginners Guide to Fix and Flip Real Estate Investing

The Ultimate Beginners Guide to Private Equity Real Estate Investing

Ultimate Beginners Guide to Real Estate Investing Financing

Building Wealth Through Real Estate - A Beginners Retirement Guide

The Ultimate Guide to Marketing for Real Estate Investors

Watch for more at www.jimpellerin.com.

About the Author

Jim Pellerin has been investing in Real Estate for over 25 years. During that time, he has conducted over $30M worth of real estate transactions.

He was the founder of several Real Estate businesses with the latest, Peller Media, focusing on providing digital marketing services for real estate professionals such as real estate agents and mortgage brokers and investors.

He has read over 700 books on subjects such as real estate investing, self development, education, cognitive psychology, marketing and sales.

He has a degree in Computer Science which he received from the University of New Brunswick in Fredericton, New Brunswick, Canada.

Read more at www.jimpellerin.com.

www.ingramcontent.com/pod-product-compliance
Lightning Source LLC
LaVergne TN
LVHW052315200926
848481LV00002B/572
* 9 7 9 8 2 2 4 7 0 7 3 4 8 *